MORALITY
AND THE
HUMAN
GOODS

An Introduction to
Natural Law Ethics

Alfonso Gómez-Lobo

GEORGETOWN UNIVERSITY PRESS / WASHINGTON, D.C.

Georgetown University Press, Washington, D.C.
© 2002 by Georgetown University Press. All rights reserved.
Printed in the United States of America

10 9 8 7 6 5 4 3 2 1   2002

This volume is printed on acid-free offset book paper.

Library of Congress Cataloging-in-Publication Data

Gómez-Lobo, Alfonso, 1940–
    Morality and the human goods : an introduction to natural law ethics /
Alfonso Gómez-Lobo.
        p. cm.
    Includes bibliographical references and index.
    ISBN 0-87840-885-1 (pbk. : alk. paper)
    1. Ethics. 2. Natural law. I. Title.

BJ1012.G645   2002
171′.2—dc21
                                                        2001040804

To my students:
past, present, future

For our inquiry is about the most important thing,
namely the good and the bad life.

Plato, Republic 578c

CONTENTS

PREFACE

To the Reader

In these pages you will find an attempt to formulate in a clear and straightforward manner a version of the mainstream tradition of moral philosophy in Western thought. This tradition usually is known as natural law ethics. (The Appendix provides an explanation of the sense in which the label "natural law" is understood in this book.) It is firmly grounded on insights first put forward by the Platonic Socrates and the mature Plato, by Aristotle and by the Stoics. Those insights were later incorporated into Judeo-Christian moral thinking and have reached us as part of sophisticated bodies of moral knowledge. St. Thomas Aquinas is a major figure in the shaping of this tradition, and his views (as well as those of modern Thomists) provide much of the inspiration for this book.

Although I do not wish to deny my debt to my immediate and remote sources (they are listed in the Appendix), I make few historical references in the body of the work. My intention is to argue for certain moral claims in their own right, independent of the point in time at which they were first conceived or defended.

What the present book contains, then, is a contemporary reconstruction of one moral theory. It is the theory that the author has come to regard not as perfect or flawless but as the most plausible one—and certainly the one that best represents what has been called our "ordinary morality" or "common moral consciousness."

The book is addressed primarily to students and readers not formally trained in philosophy who feel the need for a reliable conceptual structure for their own thinking in the midst of the confusing array of moral views expressed today. Without a relatively unified framework of moral convictions, it is virtually impossible to give direction to one's life and attain consistency in one's choices.

I trust that if you are persuaded by the arguments set forth here and, moreover, you endeavor to lead a life in successful pursuit, care, and respect of the proposed goods, you will lead a flourishing and fulfilled life—insofar as this is possible for a mortal being living in a flawed and imperfect world.

ACKNOWLEDGMENTS

I owe debts of gratitude to many people for their direct or indirect contributions to the crafting of this book. I am grateful to my colleagues in the Georgetown University philosophy department for providing a stimulating and congenial environment for intellectual inquiry. Among them, Denis Bradley has been an inexhaustible source of information and advice on traditional ethics, and Madison Powers was kind enough to discuss with me his views on the principle of double effect. I also am grateful to William McGeehan, my teaching assistant during two semesters, who sharply criticized my views at every step from his decidedly consequentialist convictions.

With regard to the manuscript itself, Alejandra Carrasco and Heath White made useful observations, Henry Richardson gave me thoughtful suggestions for the title, Walter Pfannkuche forced me to reformulate some of my claims, and Mark Murphy forwarded detailed comments on the first chapters that proved to be invaluable. Most of all, I am grateful to William Haines, who went well beyond the call of duty in his lengthy and well-thought-out criticism of the whole piece.

My warm gratitude does not entail, of course, that any of the aforementioned friends and colleagues necessarily agrees with anything I hold in this book.

Finally, I would like to extend my thanks to the members of the Ryan family of Chicago, who endowed the Ryan Chair in Metaphysics and Moral Philosophy—to which I had the honor of being appointed in 1997.

INTRODUCTION

THE ORIGINAL SETTING: PLATO'S *CRITO*

One of the oldest (and finest) examples of the practice of moral philosophy is a brief Platonic dialogue called the *Crito*. Socrates has been condemned to death by an Athenian jury on charges of not honoring the gods of the city and corrupting the young. In his defense speech (as re-created by Plato), Socrates tries to show that he is a victim of generalized Athenian prejudice against intellectuals and that the charges are both false and ill-conceived. Socrates fails, however, to persuade the jury that he is, indeed, innocent.

While Socrates is in jail awaiting execution, his friends make careful preparations to get him out of the prison and help him flee from Athens. When the execution is only one or two days away, Crito— an old friend of Socrates—conveys to him the news that everything is ready for his escape. Crito knows Socrates well enough, however, to realize that he has to give Socrates reasons to escape: He must provide Socrates with arguments that lead to the conclusion that he ought to avoid being executed.

We are not here interested in the particular arguments. We are concerned solely with the fact that arguments must be produced because Socrates is, as he says, "the kind of man who listens only to the argument (*lógos*) that on reflection seems best (to him)."[1]

Socrates later adds a further restriction to the discussion with Crito: The question of whether he should escape ought to be considered not in terms of cost, public opinion, or consequences for his children but exclusively in terms of whether it would be just—that is, morally right—to do so.[2]

That is why the *Crito* is a model case of a moral discussion; insofar as the discussion invokes principles or general moral norms, it also is a paradigm of the practice of moral philosophy. At this point, the reader may wish to read the *Crito* to decide whether Socrates' arguments are compelling, whether he shows himself to be a fool by staying and dying, or whether his choice was not only the result of his personal integrity but also reasonable and wise. These questions are indeed pertinent, but at the moment I would like to focus on the conversation itself to draw a few inferences about the practice of moral philosophy in general.

Sometimes, when people are asked to give a reply to a moral question (e.g., whether doing X is wrong), they tend to say, "But who is to decide whether it is wrong or not?" It is not unusual for them to draw a contrast between a *moral* question and a *legal* one— with the implication that the courts are empowered to give a binding reply in the legal domain, whereas there is no equivalent institution for the moral domain. The next step for someone who presses the claim that there is no ultimate institutional authority in moral matters is to say, "Who are you to tell me what I should do? You decide what's wrong for you, and I decide what's wrong for me." In other words, it is readily assumed that morality is essentially a private matter and, furthermore, relative to the individual.

The two friends in the *Crito,* naturally enough, accept that there is a distinction between the legal and the moral domain. There is no doubt that the court has settled the legal question about Socrates, but the moral question is not treated as a purely private and subjective matter. It is not the case that Socrates replies to Crito: "You have decided that I would be doing the right thing if I escape, but I, in turn, have decided that it would be wrong. It is right according to you and wrong according to me, and that's it."

To the question, "Who decides in moral matters?" the *Crito* provides a firm and clear reply: "*We* do." Morality is not a matter to be decided from the perspective of the first person singular but from the perspective of the first person plural. An agreement must be found.

Because Crito and Socrates are not in agreement, they will have to initiate a conversation in which each of them will attempt to convince the other. To persuade someone like Socrates (or any reasonable person, for that matter), you cannot appeal simply to your own first-person singular considerations. To say, "Because I feel like it (although you may not)" or "because I think it is fun (although you may not think so)" are not acceptable justifications. These utterances would come from someone who would be abandoning the effort to persuade—and thus attempting to withdraw from the conversation.

To remain a participant, you must provide a justification that goes beyond subjective feelings (which are private events) and appeals to something that is accessible to both (and all) persons. Like most moral reasoning by serious people, the argumentation in the *Crito* is public in the sense that anyone considering it carefully may find reasons to accept or reject it that are not grounded on how he or she feels. Moral justification, insofar as it is addressed to other persons (i.e., insofar as it is interpersonal), must appeal to objective reasons.

Not only are appeals to subjective feelings inadmissible within the moral conversation. Pronouncements that are based solely on the authority of the speaker also should be ruled out. "This is right (or wrong) because I say so" is unacceptable not because the wrong reasons are given but because no reasons at all are offered. There is nothing for an interlocutor to consider that might lead her justifiably to believe or disbelieve the moral claim.

In spite of what must have been his imposing personality, Socrates does not want Crito to answer contrary to Crito's own beliefs (i.e., purely on the authority of what someone else has said).[3] Socrates expects his friend to raise objections and to think for himself. The conversation, in fact, reflects a fundamentally egalitarian attitude. The persons engaging in it are on the same footing, and none can claim authority grounded on a privileged access to moral truth.

From the egalitarian character of the conversation, a further suggestion follows (which is only hinted at in the *Crito*)—namely, that the outcome of the conversation can be generalized. If it is wrong for Socrates to escape, it would be equally wrong for Crito (or anyone else) to escape in the same circumstances. To exempt oneself from this consequence would be to claim for oneself a special privilege or superior rank that contradicts the assumed equal footing of the parties. Equality of the participants leads to the claim that the results apply to anyone facing the same choice.

An interesting corollary (not mentioned in the *Crito*) of the suggestion that moral discussions can establish general claims is the so-called "Golden Rule": Do not do to others what you would not like to have done to you. If it is right for me to do something to you (e.g., to steal your wallet or your purse), then by virtue of the implied generalization it also would be right for you to do the same to me. Because I have reasons to object to your stealing my wallet or my purse, however, I have to concede that it would not be right for me in the first place to take that kind of action.

The Golden Rule is an acceptable move at this stage in the conversation because it is a way of extending its egalitarian features. Neither Socrates nor Crito would have had reasons to reject it, if they had considered it.

The lesson to be drawn from Plato's *Crito*, then, is that the "original setting" of moral philosophy is an idealized conversation in which two or more individuals give each other reasons (of the pertinent sort) to try to agree on whether a certain kind of action is generically right or wrong. They understand that the reply would be impartially binding on all of them.

We should remember, however, that Plato, the author of the *Crito*, had copies made, and that he circulated them among his friends in Athens and abroad during the first decades of the fourth century B.C. This decision allowed other people to become parties to a conversation that allegedly took place in the solitude of a prison cell. Greek readers could understand and assess the arguments; many probably did—perhaps not all of them favorably.

Thus, the initial conversation transcended the walls of the Athenian prison and became accessible to individuals who were distant in space and time. If we consider that the *Crito* can be read today not only in English but in many different languages, we can assert that the original setting allows for the inclusion of all kinds of participants in the practice of moral philosophy.

Who is included, in principle, and who is excluded from the practice or activity called "moral philosophy"? Surely the conversation is not restricted to the ancient Greeks. Through adequate translations, the arguments of the Platonic text are accessible to people everywhere. Furthermore, it would be a mistake to think that moral philosophy should be restricted, say, to males just because the characters in the dialogue are men. Women have fruitfully read the *Crito* and will continue to do so. Minorities cannot be excluded either. In principle, persons from racial or linguistic minority groups can understand the reasons given by Socrates and hence are legitimate parties to the discussion.

Nor should anyone be excluded because of his or her religious convictions. Such persons, however, are asked not to introduce claims that are based on faith (and the pronouncements of persons who have authority to teach that faith) but to argue on the basis of premises that are open to all. Acceptance by a group of persons of a premise that is based on faith (e.g., "Human beings were created by God in His image and likeness") may generate a different conversation, one called "moral theology"; we are not concerned with it here, however, because not all persons share its starting points.

Definitely excluded, on the other hand, are your dog, your cat, your favorite dolphin, and the elephant in your local zoo. Insofar as these beings cannot read the *Crito*, engage us in a critical discussion of its arguments, and acknowledge duties and responsibility for their actions, we cannot include animals (or trees or inorganic matter) as partners in our practice of moral philosophy.

There is a tendency today to put animals—at least higher mammalian vertebrates—on virtually an equal footing with humans with regard to moral standing,[4] but as the chief proponent of animal rights openly acknowledges, "Animals are not moral agents and so can have none of the duties moral agents can have."[5] We must discuss moral matters with moral agents because moral agency—the capacity to act under the guidance of the concepts of right and wrong—is indissolubly linked to the capacity to understand these abstract concepts and to accept or reject propositions in which they appear.

What about children and severely handicapped human beings? The condition of children surely is different from that of animals. Young children under favorable circumstances do become adults and hence are capable in principle of entering into the dialogue at later stages of their lives, but it is reasonable for them to be under the moral authority of their parents and tutors until the phase is reached in which they can grasp on their own the reasons given in the moral conversation. Because the original setting of moral philosophy is not limited to a specific point in time, inclusion of children in the exercise of interpersonal justification of moral claims really amounts to consideration of the replies and objections they could raise later as actual adults.

Unlike children, mentally handicapped persons are not simply immature for the time being. They are seriously deficient in a basic human characteristic. However, just as we cannot exclude in principle an uneducated person who has never read the *Crito* but could in principle read it if favorable social and economic circumstances obtained, likewise, if handicapped persons were normal human beings, they would be able, in principle, to join us. Note that this is not true of animals. If a dog who is deficient in a basic canine characteristic were a normal dog, it still could not be part of the moral conversation. A mentally handicapped person deserves as much consideration in the moral debate as an uneducated peasant from Madagascar or Bolivia, although, because of their special circumstances, none of them, as a sad matter of fact, may actually participate in the practice of moral philosophy. To take such persons into consideration entails, for example, not accepting as morally right any action that they in principle would have had reason to reject if they had had the normal capacity to discuss it with us.

Again, who decides a moral question in the sense of reaching a conclusion about where the truth lies? *We* do—and here "we" refers first to you, the reader, and to me, the writer, but then also to any human being who is capable in principle of understanding abstract moral terms and using them in articulate sentences. The "original setting," then, is this imaginary conversation in which we try to justify to each other certain moral claims by means of objective reasons.

Road Map

Although our goal is to attain agreement in moral matters, there is some territory to be covered before we get there. The treatment of the prior, foundational area is contained in chapters 1 through 5 of this book.

Chapter 1 introduces a very general principle for human action that the reader should keep in mind at all times. Chapter 2 proposes a list of goods (not moral goods, as we shall see) that jointly define human flourishing or happiness—the ultimate goal of all action. Chapter 3 attempts to answer some controversial questions that arise about the goods introduced in chapter 2. Chapter 4 formulates guidelines for the actual attainment of goods, some of which provide the link between the foundational and the specifically moral domain.

Chapter 5 interrupts the flow of the conversation to examine the questions that should be raised if we want to understand a specific human action. Explaining the key features of an action is primarily a descriptive task that contributes to moral thought by providing a focus for passing moral judgment.

Because passing moral judgment requires moral norms, chapter 6 presents a sketch of such norms and a strategy to justify them on the basis of the foundational material. Chapters 7 and 8 apply the justified norms to two passionately disputed kinds of action: abortion and euthanasia. In the epilogue (chapter 9), an effort is made to draw some further contrasts between the system presented in this book and the theories of utilitarianism and moral libertarianism.

Occasionally an author will indicate which chapters of his work can be skipped without significant loss for the reader. The present book, however, constitutes a single extended argument within which every step counts. It is fair to suggest, however, that if a reader has gone through it once and would like to go back to the essentials of the theory, she will find them in chapters 1, 2, 4, and 6.

Let us now proceed to the starting point of our conversation.

Notes

1. *Crito* 46b.
2. *Crito* 48b–c.
3. *Crito* 49d.
4. Singer (1975).
5. Regan (1983), 357, quoted in Regan (1993), 352.

ONE

A First Principle

Any attempt to reason with other human beings has to start somewhere. If I can show you that statement Q logically follows from statement P, and I get you to agree that P is true, then I am in a position to persuade you that Q is also true. In this case, our agreement on P is an adequate starting point.

Arguments within a conversation usually follow this pattern, and the *Crito* is no exception. To get Crito to agree with his conclusion, Socrates has to get him to agree first on one or more statements from which his conclusion (that it would be wrong for him to escape) follows.

The purpose of this chapter is to invite you, the reader, to agree on something that will allow us to make further progress. If we do not agree on anything, you would be well-advised to close this book and throw it in the trash (or sell it second-hand to diminish your losses).

Perhaps you will agree that, in general, it makes sense to refrain from eating food that smells bad. If it smells bad, it is probably spoiled, and you want to avoid the ensuing sickness. You also may agree that exercising regularly is something worth doing (although, in real life, you may well be a couch potato). I may ask, however, "Why is it worthwhile?" And you will probably answer, "Because it keeps you in good health."

We seem to be starting to agree on two things here: that it is bad to be sick and good to be healthy and that it is reasonable to avoid being sick and to try to stay healthy.

Illness is not the only bad thing for us, nor is health the only good one. We are surrounded by many good and bad things, so the normal attitude toward sickness and health reasonably can be adopted toward other things.

Hence, I suggest that we agree on the following, which I call "The Formal Principle" (FP):

One should pursue what is good, and one should avoid what is bad.

Several things must be said about this principle before we continue. The verbs ("to pursue," "to avoid") should be taken to stand for a wide variety of actions. The former can be replaced by, for example, "try to obtain," "secure," "do," "foster," "perform," and so forth, the latter by "to refrain from," "eschew," "shun," "run away from," and so forth. These verbs describe actions that we humans deliberately perform as a result of taking a positive or a negative stand toward something. The reasons to take a positive or a negative stand, to do or to refrain from doing something, are encapsulated in the words "good" and "bad," respectively.

How are the terms "good" and "bad" being used here? They are surely evaluative terms. If one values something, one says it is good; contrariwise, we say it is bad. The evaluation we are considering here is the usual nonmoral evaluation: Illness and health are not morally bad and morally good things, respectively. We are implicitly appealing to this principle whenever we exhort someone to go to a good college, avoid bad grades, buy a good pair of sneakers, get rid of a bad car, and so forth.

The FP, therefore, is not a moral principle but a general principle of practical rationality. In the absence of further specifications, it cannot tell us whether some action is morally right or wrong. Because of its generality, it also leaves open whose good ought to be pursued and when. Sometimes it will be rational for me to pursue my good, sometimes the good of someone else. The principle does not enjoin me to actively pursue on each occasion every single good that is within my grasp. What the principle rejects in broad terms is the pursuit of something bad (for anyone) and the deliberate neglect of something good (for someone). By itself, the principle does not resolve practical conflicts.

The term "practical" is not meant here in its standard sense (where "practical" means the same as "useful," "capable of being put to immediate use"). I am relying heavily on the Greek roots of the term.

The adjective "practical" is derived from *praxis,* the Greek word for "action." This is why in philosophy it has been used to mean "pertaining to human action." "Practical reason," then, stands for our capacity to use our rational powers to guide us in what we *do* as opposed to what we *make* or what we *figure out* without any intention of putting it into practice. Aristotle called these two further uses of reason "productive reason" and "theoretical reason," respectively.[1]

To say that we have just formulated a principle for practical rationality is not to claim that all human action conforms to it but that all human action *ought* to conform to it. To pursue something that is not good or to avoid something that is indeed good is possible, even quite common, but it is irrational. If smoking is bad for your health, then according to the basic principle of practical rationality, it is generally irrational to smoke. If polluting rivers is bad for those who live close to them, it is generally irrational to pollute rivers. In particular instances, however, there may be a compensating good (such as the relaxation some people seem to derive from smoking or the preservation of jobs if a certain factory had to close if it couldn't pollute at all) that may lead us to revise the charge of irrationality.

Can we agree, though, that the principle of practical rationality is true?

Let us examine first what we are doing. We do not intend to say that it is true *because* we agree on it. Two persons may agree that Philadelphia is the capital of Pennsylvania. This assertion is false, however, and their agreement will not make it true.

The grounding move should go in the opposite direction. Ideally, we should agree on something *because it is true.* Therefore, our efforts in search of agreements should aim at finding reasons to think that what we agree on is indeed true. If we have doubts about agreeing that Harrisburg is the capital of Pennsylvania, we may want to find out, say, whether the state legislature meets there.

What reasons do we have to think that it is true that we should pursue what is good and avoid what is bad? Surely no observation of empirical facts will provide us with such reasons because the claim itself is not an empirical claim. It is not a claim about the world and our experience of it. By "empirical claim" we mean a statement that can be known to be true (or false) by observation and experimentation. Typically, chemistry makes empirical claims, and that is why chemistry students need to conduct experiments and observe their results. There are no labs for ethics courses.

The first principle of practical reason does not make a claim about the world of nature, nor about cities and their institutional roles. It does not make a claim about the world at all. As we have seen, it makes a claim about how we should act. It tells us that if something is good, it is rational to pursue it, and if it is bad, it is rational to avoid it.

What if a person denies this principle and tells us that X is bad for her but that it is OK for her to pursue X? We have several options for an explanation.

(1) It may be the case that X is bad for her but that it is conducive to Y and that Y is indeed good for her. It is bad to have a leg amputated, but if that is going to save her life, it is rational to go ahead with the amputation. Considered in isolation, an amputation surely is bad for anyone. In the foregoing example, however, it is not really bad, all things considered, because of the condition of the person's leg. In fact, the amputation is instrumentally good. Hence, the principle has not been rejected: The action in our example is perfectly rational under the requirements of the principle itself.

(2) Alternatively, we might find that the person is deranged. Because the principle provides criteria for rationality, her rejection of it (together with a host of other symptoms) may reveal to a psychiatrist that the patient is indeed out of her wits. Pursuit of what is bad for oneself, or consistently self-destructive choices, constitute the kind of behavior that psychiatric clinics are designed to prevent. We have not been shown that the principle is false, only that consistent noncompliance with it is an indication of a serious psychological disorder. Note that occasional noncompliance is quite normal. We often make irrational choices, but this does not entail that we are rejecting the truth of the principle. It only shows that it is a normative principle, not a descriptive one.

(3) A third explanation of why someone might think it is rational to pursue something bad may not appear to be very plausible; yet, as we shall see, it will point us in the right direction. In Greek, two of the several terms for "good" and "bad" are *kalón* and *kakón*, respectively. Because the two words are somewhat

similar to each other, we can imagine a student confusing the two words during the first weeks of language instruction and saying "X is *kakón*" when she really means the opposite. Again, the principle has not been denied because "X is *kakón,* and you ought to pursue X" is not a counterexample to the principle, given what the student means by *kakón.*

The explanation of why the student makes the paradoxical claim (she has misunderstood the Greek adjective) provides an important clue because it allows us to understand why it is odd to say that it is rational to pursue something bad, if that is what we really mean.

The oddity is related to the fact that the English term "bad" (like its equivalents in other languages) is used to qualify something that is worth avoiding. Conversely, "good" is used to commend something as worth pursuing. Therefore, to deny the principle of practical rationality is to say something inconsistent with the very meaning of its key terms. It is analogous to holding that a bachelor is a married man.

The first principle of practical rationality, therefore, is true by virtue of the meaning of its terms. Any person who understands what we are talking about when we say (in any language) that something is good should be able to realize that the principle is true and hence have no objection to our positing it as the first step in our moral philosophy.

If the truth of the principle is analogous to that of the statement that a bachelor is an unmarried male, we can immediately see that, by itself, it is not very helpful. To know that all bachelors are unmarried males does not tell a woman at a party which of the three men talking to her is, in fact, a bachelor. Likewise, to have the basic practical understanding that good things are the things worth pursuing does not tell us which things are indeed good for myself or for other people.

To flag this insufficiency, I qualify the principle under consideration by saying that it is a *formal* principle. I mean by this that it does not provide us with actual criteria to determine which things are good. Thus, it is analogous to the claim that if this creature swimming under my boat is a whale, it is a mammal. This is true, of course, but it does not tell me whether the creature is a whale or not.

Note

1. Aristotle *Metaphysics* 6.1.1025b25.

TWO

Supplementary Principles of Practical Rationality: Basic Human Goods

In our attempt to engage in the conversation called "moral philosophy," we have agreed, I trust, on FP, the Formal Principle for rationality in action, and we have agreed because we have found reasons to think that it is true. The meanings of its key terms have convinced us that it cannot be false. If we are willing to call *good* a thing that is worth pursuing, it cannot be false to say that, as rational beings, we are justified in pursuing it.

The next questions you naturally will ask are: Which things are good? How can you tell a good from a bad thing? Moreover, good for whom?

These are very difficult questions that have been vigorously disputed since the days of Socrates and perhaps even before. We all want to know what is, or will turn out to be, good for us. If we would know in advance that a trip is going to be disastrous for us, we would not undertake it. If we knew in advance the number of the winning lottery ticket, we would purchase it (in accordance with the FP, of course).

There is, then, a first obstacle to be faced in the identification of goods: our ignorance of the future. We can bet on future outcomes, we can make reasonable guesses on the basis of past experience, we can take the right steps towards a desired goal, but we can never be absolutely sure.

A second obstacle lying on our way has been mentioned already: We are surrounded by a vast amount of goods. In fact, most things (perhaps all things) have a good side to them. There is always something that makes them attractive, and sometimes the attraction ends up being outweighed by the inconveniences that follow—like the upset stomach following the overabundant meal. Sometimes things are outright deceptive, like the "lemon" a car dealer tries to sell you. It is a beautiful, bright red convertible, but it will fall apart within a few days.

Thus, many goods are "apparent goods" only. Their attractive side hides their defects. What we want, obviously, are the real goods—the goods that appear good and are not defective in relevant respects.

By introducing the distinction between apparent goods and real goods, I have already made a preemptive move against a position that is widely held today but also was known to the ancient Greeks. I mean the subjectivist position already hinted at in chapter 1.

With regard to goods, the Subjectivist Thesis (ST) could be formulated thus:

If X seems to A to be good, then X is good for (beneficial to) A.

At first sight this position is attractive because it deals primarily with the concerns of the individual person and seems to preserve a valuable autonomy for her. By "autonomy" here I understand the privilege of individuals to determine and to choose their own good without paternalistic interference from others.

I plan to deal later with the choice aspect of autonomy. The ST addresses only the determination aspect: I determine what is good for me; you determine what is good for you! "I don't want anyone to tell me what's good for me" is a remark we often hear (or make ourselves). This all sounds like a commendable pitch for individualism, but it just isn't true. What seems good to me may actually not be good for me simply because I can make mistakes. Indeed, one of the most notorious domains for self-deception is that of one's own good. When I want something badly, I have little trouble convincing myself that it will be for my own good. Some people are known for buying beautiful, bright red "lemons."

It may well be the case that someone else is in an even worse position than myself to know what would be good for me or in my best interest. I may be better situated in general to pass a judgment of this sort, but anyone who admits that such a judgment *can* go wrong (i.e., that what seems good to a person is not always good for that person) has granted that the ST is false.

I can still say that I made a mistake, but it is *my* mistake, and doubtless there is value in this attitude. Rationality, however, demands that I pursue what is good, not just what seems good; therefore, once I acknowledge that I can make mistakes, I see that rationality demands that I try to find and correct any mistakes I may be making.

What can we do to avoid mistakes in this all-important domain? How are we to discern when something is a real good or only an apparent good?

What we need is a criterion. We use the word "criterion" metaphorically for anything that functions like a sieve or a strainer—that is, for an instrument that allows us to separate, say, larger pebbles from smaller ones, or liquids from solids.

Is it realistic to expect to discover one (and only one) criterion to distinguish the good things from the bad things, especially those that appear to be good? Some philosophers have answered this question in the affirmative and have produced a candidate. British philosopher Jeremy Bentham, for example, held that pleasure itself is good and that it can function as a criterion to determine derivative instances of good. If something is pleasant in itself or the cause or instrument of pleasure, it is good or valuable.

There are various difficulties involved in this view, the most important of which has to do with the very notion of pleasure. We shall deal with this issue later. At present I would like to cast some doubt on the prospect of finding a single criterion for goodness. If we look around, we will see that the many good things that surround us differ considerably from each other. There are good cars, good classes, good vacations, good museums, good friends, and so forth. We praise all these things by characterizing them as good, but if we are asked to say why the Metropolitan Museum in New York is a good museum and a Mercedes-Benz is a good car, we will give quite different answers. It would be intolerably vague and unsatisfactory to say that both provide pleasure. In one case we will mention certain works of art to be seen there, in the second perhaps the durability of its engine. The pleasant feeling experienced by people who visit the former and drive the latter does not tell us much about the goodness of either one.

The criteria (note the plural form) differ widely from one class of things to the next. There is no single criterion of goodness across all classes. Likewise, there is no reason to expect that fundamental human goods can be discerned by applying a single criterion. Hence, my strategy will be to assume that there is a plurality of criteria and then question the view that they are all reducible to one.

Criteria often are articulated by means of general propositions that can be used as premises for inferences. Let me provide an example: "Any number that is divisible by 2 is an even number." This proposition functions as a starting point for the following inference: "The number 6 is a particular instance of a number divisible by 2; therefore, 6 is an even number."

I plan to adopt a similar pattern for the criteria that should allow us to distinguish real goods from apparent goods. This pattern will be as follows:

X is a basic human good, and if Y is an instance of X, then Y is a real good.

The challenge is to find the correct substitutions for X. They have to be general terms that stand for things that are basic ingredients of human flourishing. A basic human good is to the good life roughly as pasta is to an Italian meal. Pasta is one of its key ingredients, and it can appear under many particular guises (spaghetti, fettucine, tortellini, etc.). Just as a meal without any pasta is unlikely to qualify as a product of Italian cooking, a life that is totally lacking in one or more of the basic human goods can hardly be said to be an excellent one.

I will present my candidates for basic goods; you must decide whether you agree with my list. I will have to give you reasons to agree (recall the nature of moral philosophy as a rational discussion among people regarded as equals); reasons will be difficult to provide, however, because, for the most part, one cannot appeal to something more universal than each basic good. Occasionally, I will appeal to the ordinary notion of "being well off." I plan to do this in cases that I expect to be fairly uncontroversial and thus capable of commanding wide-ranging assent.

On the other hand, to invoke the meanings of the terms involved (as I did in the case of the FP) to justify the truth of each principle certainly would be illegitimate. The situation is analogous to that of the woman from a previous example. As you may recall, she knows by virtue of the meaning of the term "bachelor" that a bachelor is an unmarried male, but if she wants to get anywhere she has to make a further assessment and say, "The nice guy offering me a drink is a bachelor." This statement may be false—but if it is true, it is not true by virtue of the meaning of the expressions "bachelor" and "the nice guy offering me a drink." The reasons to think that it is true must be nonlinguistic: Maybe he is the only one of the three not wearing a wedding band, or perhaps she finds out from someone who has known him for years that he is not married. At any rate, the meaning of words here is not enough.

We know how we should *not* argue. How we *should* argue is best shown by simply doing it. Let us start with something truly basic:

(P.1) Life is a basic human good.

By "life" I mean here human life at the basic biological level, manifesting itself in the typical functions of a human organism (taking nourishment, growing, etc.). Whether a certain organism is human depends on whether it has the complete set of standard human chromosomes or a deviation therefrom that counts as a human genetic abnormality. An egg or a sperm by itself does not qualify. Neither of them, as we now know, has the complete set. It also matters whether it is a complete organism with its own self-developing life and not just a part of one. A toe or a tumor or some drops of blood do have cells each of which has the required chromosomes, but none of them is a complete organism.

I am not a biologist, and these definitions are probably vague and inadequate for rigorous scientific study. They are sufficient, however, to understand what happens when someone dies: There is a cessation of basic biological functions, and because of that there also is a cessation of every other, higher function. As human beings, we are all sustained by the wonderfully complex (and fragile) system of functions that are performed, for the most part unconsciously, in our bodies.

These are all descriptive statements and therefore not strictly part of moral philosophy. Let us make the transition into the latter by placing our consideration of these matters under the concepts of good and bad.

Would you consent, as you read this page, that your life be taken? I suspect you would not. You probably think, as I do, that death is awful—whether it is your own death or that of your boyfriend, your girlfriend, your spouse, your child, your mother, or. . . . The list can go on indefinitely. You can agree that even the execution of a murderer is a terrible thing; if you are in favor of the death penalty, you would add that something so terrible is precisely what that individual deserves. Death, with its implication of one's final dissolution and annihilation, is the ultimate evil, the ultimate thing we wish to avoid.

By contrast, life appears to be a good worth enjoying and celebrating, as we implicitly acknowledge when we celebrate our own and other peoples' birthdays.

Life is not the sole good (we can possess many other goods beyond being merely alive), but it is surely the very first one. Without it we cannot partake in any other goods. In this sense, it is the grounding good. It also is worth having on its own: It is good to be alive. The closest analogy to this claim is that health also is good in the same way: When we are not ill we can pursue other goods, but being healthy is just plain good in itself.

I am sure that you can easily come up with an objection that is gaining social acceptance today because it underpins arguments for voluntary euthanasia and physician-assisted suicide: There are people for whom life is simply bad. We will explore the morality of euthanasia later. Right now what matters is whether it is true that life is good, even if for a few people life appears to be bad.

Why do some people regard their lives as bad? Why do some people long to die? What makes life bad surely is one or more of the following: chronic illness, acute physical pain, extreme poverty and destitution, being lonely and forsaken by friends and relatives, realizing that one has committed a terrible crime (like Oedipus, who killed his father and married his mother), or experiencing unrequited love or clinical depression. You may add to the list as you see fit.

The list is necessary, however, because without reference to items such as these one would be at a loss to understand how a person could regard her life as bad. If by fiat one could do away with illness, pain, poverty, and so forth, would it be sensible to say that life itself is bad for that person? Surely not, because, strictly speaking, it is not life that is bad (unless perhaps "life" is understood in a different, not strictly biological sense). The illness, pain, poverty, and so forth are the bad things. Life as such is different from those evils, and one cannot conclude that in its own right it is an evil.

Perhaps, however, life is a purely neutral thing that derives all of its value or disvalue from other goods. To prove that B has derivative or instrumental value, one must show that B is instrumental in attaining A and that A has intrinsic value. Assume, however, that B sometimes can be instrumental to the attainment of C. If one shows that C is bad, one will have shown in turn that B also is instrumentally bad. B, then, will be instrumentally both good and bad, but in itself neither (this is exactly what "neutral" means).

How can we persuade each other that something has intrinsic value? If we have reason to agree that G is intrinsically good and that D, E, and F are neither extrinsically nor instrumentally conducive to G but are internal constituents of G, we also have reason to think that they are intrinsically valuable. We all doubtless agree that happiness or the good life is the ultimate worthwhile thing—something that we value not because it will lead to something else but because it is good itself. Surely life is not external or instrumental to the good life. The good life is not a product or a consequence of life. It is life fully realized. Life, then—as the key ingredient of the good life (though not the only one)—is worth having for its own sake. Life is not neutral, nor is death. Death is totally incompatible with the ultimate goal of human beings.

I submit further that the admission that life is a basic good underlies many of our common convictions—such as regarding murder as the most serious crime, regardless of how the victim fares with regard to other goods. Indeed, the value of life hitherto has been the cornerstone of all our values.

This view is quite widespread. We live surrounded by institutions, facilities, vehicles, and instruments that can be understood only on the basis of the collective conviction that death is the ultimate evil for anyone and life the first good. Otherwise, what is the point of having emergency rooms, ambulances, rescue helicopters, oxygen tubes, and so forth?

As I have just mentioned, there is a good that is closely connected with life and analogous to it: the good of health. This good, in turn, manifests itself in other worthwhile bodily operations such as perceiving, sensing, and moving on one's own.

Health does not play a strictly grounding role, however, because it is possible to be in poor health and yet enjoy other, nonbodily goods (such as the friendship of those caring for you with love and devotion), although a life lived for the most part in good health will be better than one with long periods of illness. For most people (including you, I trust), it is indeed axiomatic that health is something good. By "axiomatic" I mean "akin to the axioms of geometry" (i.e., to propositions that are readily accepted as true without proof).

In fact, before introducing the principle of practical rationality in chapter 1, I appealed to your intuitions about health and sickness. It goes without saying that illness causes so many impediments, annoyances, expenses, and other problems that a reasonable person will concede without hesitation that one is better off when one is in good health because of its instrumental value.

Yet there also seems to be an intrinsic value in health that is hard to deny. Health, by itself, is worth having as an ingredient of a flourishing life. Again, we can point to medical schools, hospitals, pharmacies, smoking bans, and so forth to show that there is a social commitment to the good of health.

Beyond the preservation of life and the promotion of health, most people also would grant that the healthy transmission of life is valuable. This realization leads us to a second item in our list of basic goods:

(P.2) The family is a basic human good.

Here we enter a controversial and complex subject. The family is a matter of vigorous controversy mainly because marriages fail today at an astonishing rate. There also is the charge that it is inevitably a patriarchal, male-dominated institution that is detrimental to the well-being of women, which can be replaced by new arrangements, such as single-parent households. We often hear too about parents whose children have made them suffer a lot and children whose abusive parents have made *them* suffer quite a bit. You may remember the old bumper-sticker: "Live long enough to be a burden for your children." How can the family be all that good?

One also could challenge the idea of listing the family as a *basic* good from a different perspective. There are many people who, as a matter of fact, do not have a family and seem to be doing fine, and there are religious persons—notably Roman Catholic men and women—who decline to have a family in spite of their being committed to an ethical outlook that is very much like the one presented in this book.

Let us not lose sight of our strategy and ask not factual questions but evaluative ones. Is a child better off being raised in an orphanage or in a family? Is an adult better off having a loving spouse with whom to have sex, children, companionship, fun, and common projects or being alone? Is a senior citizen better off having an affectionate daughter to drive her to a chemotherapy session or having to drive herself in spite of the pain and the nausea?

What makes the family a basic good is that in the hypothetical absence of any family ties, in the total deprivation of a loving spouse and close relatives, in the case of a life starting in an orphanage and ending in solitude, one can hardly speak of a fully flourishing existence. What makes the family a basic good is its contribution to the good life. Just as the fact that we are sometimes sick does not contradict the claim that health is a basic good, likewise failure in family life or simply not having a family (either by design or by the circumstances of life) do not entail that it would not be good to have one.

The reflection on family failure discloses an important aspect of the complex human good we are analyzing. Family life fails when other goods are missing—notably the excellence of communities that Aristotle calls *philia*, "friendship."[1] If spouses are not good friends and lovers of each other, if parents are not good friends of their children or the children of their parents, or the siblings among themselves, families fall apart. Familial friendship is to the family what health is to the body. You can cope with illness or lack of love, but you would be better off if you were in the opposite condition.

The family, then, with its key ingredients of love, sex, procreation, mothering and fathering, interaction with one's kin, and mutual support, is a basic good that we have reason to wish for ourselves and others.

We do not live only in families, however. When a young person leaves for college, she leaves home to enter into a different kind of community, or more than one. As you and I understand it, leaving home is not equivalent to opting out of the family. A student remains a member of her family; any person remains a member of a family although it may be far away. What if all of one's relatives die? That is very sad indeed, but it helps most of us realize the importance of the human good of friendship beyond the family.

Hence, the next supplementary principle will be as follows:

(P.3) Friendship is a basic human good.

As we have seen, there is an inevitable overlap with the previous good, but now we are going explicitly beyond the narrow confines of the family.

In college one joins a team, volunteers with a group of people to help out in inner city schools, develops a project with students in the same major, is part of the university as a whole. These are all communities or forms of association that are brought together by a common goal.

Are you better off joining them, or not? Well, it depends. You have to examine whether you may be spreading yourself too thin and neglecting your studies. The pursuit of a certain good cannot be something automatic. You have to look at the whole context because there might be a host of goods laying claim on you. Discerning effectively among them is in turn a good, which will be discussed later.

To be on firmer ground with regard to the good now considered, I ask you to examine a narrower form of relationship: the one that coincides with our ordinary use of the term "friendship." By this I mean the kind of relationship that develops between you and a small number of people you are willing to see every day, hang out with, help when they need you, seek help from when you need them. To such people we open our hearts; we tell them what burdens us; we phone them when we have good news. These are the persons we are willing to call "friends."

Three things seem to be core ingredients of this form of relationship. First, there is affection involved (though not intense, erotic affection). We like these people; we feel comfortable with them. Second, there has to be reciprocity. I may like someone, but if that other person is unaware of me or is not willing to spend time with me or does not open his or her heart to me, I would not say we are friends. Third, friends are individuals who wish the best for each other; moreover, each does it for the other's sake. Asking for favors and never returning them or outright ill will toward a person are clear signs that friendship has vanished or has never existed.

This third ingredient makes general agreement on this human good much easier to secure than on others. If a friend is someone who wishes you well, who wants you to secure good things and not bad ones, how can you deny that friendship is good for you? Furthermore, how can it not be good to have friends, simply because they are friends, even if few opportunities arise for them to act on those wishes and be of service to you? Is it possible to think for a moment about the nature of friendship and deny that it is intrinsically and instrumentally good? Friends are a decisive component of the good life of an individual and an important resource for his securing some of his more immediate ends.

Because friendship requires more than one person and entails mutual good will, it follows that friendship also is a good of communities. The forms and rituals of friendship may vary from culture to culture (some cultures, for example, require a formal declaration of the newly established friendship), but its beneficial effect is common to all of those forms.

Without friendship, relations within a community may descend to the level of mere justice—that is, mutual respect for each other's rights without much enthusiasm for the welfare of others. Loss of the affection that goes along with friendship is the loss of something important, however. When even justice is lost—when cheating, deception, rivalry, discrimination, domination, or hatred prevail—communities tend to fall apart, and their members usually are harmed. This is not the same as the dissolution of a community when its goal is no longer sought. A tennis club may decide to liquidate its assets if no one wants to play tennis any longer, but sometimes a community is destroyed in spite of the fact that its members would like to continue to pursue the common goal. Think of a successful law firm that breaks up because two of the partners have an acrimonious fight.

In the narrow sense, then, friendship certainly is a good. We also are better off when friendship prevails in the broader communities in which we participate, all the way up to the political community (the Greeks regarded the loss of civic friendship as one of the great evils of their time). No doubt we also should include even the international community. Wars are not good for anyone (not even for those who make money selling arms, I would argue).

Communities also are connected to two other basic goods that may be considered jointly.

(P.4) Work and play are basic human goods.

By "work" I mean the myriad activities by means of which human beings produce goods and services for each other and thus earn their living. I emphasize that work can take many different forms in our culture, as well as across cultures. A man begging on a street corner is not working, but a man playing the guitar may be. If his performance is appreciated, people will give him a few coins. A service has been rendered, and a reward has been reaped.

Work often is not very pleasant. Many people hate their jobs. Some jobs do not pay much, and people want to get out of them. Most people love to see their vacation approaching. How can it be true that work is a basic human good?

As usual, it pays to tackle the question from the opposite end. Is it good to be laid off? Is it good to go through a lengthy period of unemployment?

Unemployment usually means not having an income, and that is surely bad. We need quite a bit of material things not just to make life pleasant but even to survive at a low standard of living. If you are single and a convinced ascetic, it is bad enough not to have enough money, say, for food and transportation. If you have a family, however, it is simply terrible because you see your loved ones suffering.

Isn't the loss of income the really bad thing, therefore, not the unemployment itself? Assume that you live in a country where there are unemployment benefits (remember that most people in the world do *not* have such benefits). In those circumstances, would you be better off not having a job than having one? I think not. Income is important, but it is not the decisive factor. We have all heard about the depression that can hit very rich people who do not need to make a living and hence are not forced to seek a meaningful activity. (Warning: Being a millionaire can be dangerous to your mental health!)

The key ingredient that makes work (including schoolwork) a human good seems to be the experience of achievement and self-realization that is at its very core. At work we activate at least some of our talents, and this is a source of personal satisfaction. Because volunteer work can contribute to these grounds of self-esteem, one can hold that remuneration is not essential to the goodness of work. For most of us, however, a paycheck at the end of the month also is vital.

Another important aspect of work is that it links us to our communities. We do not work alone. Most of us work within institutions—such as corporations, federal agencies, small companies, professional basketball teams, or philosophy departments—but even the most isolated producer has to sell her products to someone. Her wares or services have to be appreciated by other human beings. Work, then, puts us in contact with various communities. We make a contribution to them, and we get something in return, in the form of a salary or gratitude and recognition. Volunteers get only the latter, but they are not deprived of the core goods of work.

We may agree that work is good and unemployment bad. Does this entail that it would be sensible to make work the supreme value in our lives? Should we think highly of the fanatic, relentless workaholic? I myself do not.

There is value in relaxation—in doing something just for the fun of it. If you never take time off from work, go out to shoot baskets with your friends, swim at a local beach, go with a kid to fly a kite, or . . . the list can be very long! I try to capture it by means of the label "play."

If the forms of friendship may vary from one culture to the next, those of play vary even more. The forms of play invented by mankind are astonishingly varied. Some entail competition, others do not; some are highly regimented (e.g., chess), some are totally unstructured; some are very serious, whereas some entail humor and laughter. When you see something unproductive performed with great gusto (e.g., a neighborhood group performing a comedy or Irish dances), you are surely facing an instance of play.

The infinite variety of forms of play should not distract us from the claim that it represents an important aspect of human fulfillment. Although play seems to be the direct opposite of work, it ends up as work's natural complement. A life of work without play is hardly attractive, but neither is a life of play without work. Without work, the relaxation aspect of play probably would be lost—and with it a key reason to engage in play.

Some people in their work and in their play aim at a goal that leads us to our next item: the production of beauty.

(P.5) The experience of beauty is a basic human good.

Again, we are facing a vast domain. There is, of course, the active production of beauty (a task that is carried out primarily by artists) and the passive enjoyment of the aesthetic experience (an activity that is open to anyone).

Beauty comes in so many forms—in nature and in the works crafted by human hands—that it is simply impossible to canvass all of its different manifestations. Indeed, any object, gesture, shade of color, or musical performance can display beauty, and a second look often is needed for us to realize that it is there. In a sense, the history of art is the progressive discovery of beauty where at first no one thought it could be found. Most of what was produced by the modern industrial revolution initially was perceived as ugly until, among others, the first photographers started to show the astonishing aesthetic qualities of cranes and machines, pipes and towers. Something similar can be said about the progression in music from classical to romantic to contemporary to jazz to rock, etc. (I add "etc." because of my own limitations in this area, but you can supply your favorite new releases).

The possibilities are endless. What I invite agreement on is the claim that lives are enriched by the experience of beauty (any form thereof) and that lives without it are surely less desirable.

The aesthetic experience is sometimes obtained almost at the pure level of perception—as when the road we are traveling on makes a turn around a mountain and we are suddenly facing a vast and beautiful landscape. It is hard not to feel an immediate satisfaction in its contemplation. Sometimes, however, the experience of beauty requires considerable spade work. Enjoying Homer in Greek, Dostoevsky in Russian, or even Shakespeare (in English, of course) is possible only for people who have invested time and energy in the kind of knowledge that allows the beauty of these authors' masterpieces to shine through.

It seems to be good to know more than one language because they can give us access to the good of aesthetic experience. We should not be so specific, however. Most people have enough beauty to experience without knowledge of a foreign language. Can they live fulfilled lives, however, without any knowledge whatsoever?

I start, as usual, with a bold generalization and then try to justify it.

(P.6) Knowledge is a basic human good.

The target of inquiry and knowledge is truth. If you are going through this book with a critical eye—if you are trying to find errors or mistakes, if you wish to know whether its claims are true or not—you are already granting that truth is valuable, that it is a good.

As a student you have become a sort of professional seeker of truth, but what about people who are not fortunate enough to be in college? Do they care about knowledge and truth?

Maybe they do not care about an abstruse theory in chemistry or what your professor said about the foreign policy of France or Iraq. Does this fact entail that they do not care about knowledge at all or that knowledge is of no value for certain people?

We should remind ourselves that, as in the case of the foregoing goods, we are at a very high level of generality. The claim that work, play, and beauty are goods is cross-cultural in the sense that no restrictions are placed on the particular forms they may take. Work and play can be very different for a Tibetan farmer and for a young American computer programmer. The point is simply that these persons are better off if part of what they do can be conceived as work and part of it as play.

We can know many things, but we are not equally interested in being acquainted with all possible items of knowledge, particularly in an era of technological explosion of information. We are more eager to know some things than other things. If we try to identify the things that all of us are most interested in, a reasonable beginning can be to say that we would like to know what is good for us and what is bad for us. Again, this knowledge clearly is cross-cultural.

The reason for the widely shared appreciation of insight into what will benefit us and what will harm us is that all human beings are agents. We cannot sit idly. We have to do things, and we have to choose to do X or Y. Moreover, as we have seen, our choices will be rational if we choose what we correctly determine to be good for us.

Because we could be mistaken, which could have dire consequences for us, we want to *know* whether X is good for us. Knowledge of goods for action expressed by means of standard evaluative propositions can be labeled "practical knowledge," and we are thus justified in claiming that

(P.6a) Practical knowledge is a basic human good.

This good is about other goods. The purpose of engaging in the practice of practical knowledge is to identify the remaining human goods, generically and specifically, and to develop strategies to attain them. An example of practical knowledge would be to realize generically how important friendship is for life and to develop a good eye to choose one's friends among a crowd of acquaintances. Nourishing an already initiated friendship also requires some kind of policy—such as, for instance, postponing instant gratification to be available to attend to one's friend's needs. To realize this (and to act on it) is also to be practically smart.

Sometimes one also wants to know things that do not have an immediate impact on one's decisions. It would be good to know more about the history of India or the latest discoveries in molecular biology—perhaps not for me, but in general. I am aware of the fact that many sciences and theories are beyond my reach, but if I turn to the other extreme I can make a reliable evaluation: Am I better off if I am ignorant—if I am muddled in my thoughts about the world, its basic structures, its wide variety of manifestations? Isn't theoretical knowledge (whether it will have an impact on technology later on or not) something that fulfills us as human beings? If so, then

(P.6b) Theoretical knowledge is a basic human good.

This claim, like each of the previous claims, is quite general. Theoretical knowledge is understood here broadly and in opposition to practical knowledge. It embraces all forms of descriptive knowledge, ranging from knowledge of particular facts to the most abstract scientific and philosophical theories. The key to the distinction is that theoretical knowledge is pursued for its own sake, whereas practical knowledge is pursued for the sake of action. Typically, a theoretical proposition states something about the world as it is, whereas a practical proposition will include an evaluative or normative component (expressed by terms such as "good," "right," and similar words) that endows it with action-guiding force.

Not every instance of theoretical knowledge is a reasonable object of pursuit for me given the claim that other, more pressing, goods make on my time and resources. Sometimes I have to rest content in the awareness that it would be good to know something I will never get to know—for example, the latest discoveries in astrophysics.

What if someone denies that knowledge, at least of the theoretical sort, is a basic good? The person who issues this denial seems to be trapped in an inevitable paradox, for to deny that knowledge is a good is to claim that it is true that knowledge is not a good. This claim surely betrays an interest in the truth and a willingness to avoid error. To thus value truth over error, however, is to conceive of knowledge as a better state than ignorance. Indeed, any truth claim— any claim that one is right about something (and someone else is wrong)—is a claim that assumes the goodness of knowledge.

A more serious challenge to this view comes from those who agree that knowledge is generally a good but that in certain particular cases it is better not to know than to know because it would be painful to know. One such scenario is the case of a patient whose physician has diagnosed her as being terminally ill. I submit that knowledge of the fact that one is ill, as well as theoretical awareness of the features and stages of the illness, is better than ignorance; it is something worth having by virtue of the fact that it satisfies one's curiosity and on account of some of its practical implications. There is less of the fear caused by uncertainty, and there is so much one would like to be able to settle before dying: There are friends to talk to, grudges to smooth, and opportunities for reconciliation to be sought. All of these, I should think, are good things for a human being that are made possible by knowledge of the descriptive (i.e., theoretical) sort.

A similar scenario for the preference of ignorance over truth is that of the deceived friend or spouse. Again, I would claim that, in spite of the suffering and the pain, one is better off knowing the plain facts than being kept in the dark. If you know you have been deceived, you can make a fresh start. Deceptions tend to poison relationships in any case. In these cases, it is true, there often is a will not to know. There is a strong tendency to self-deception. For the most part, however, the choice not to know, paradoxically enough, is grounded on the truth. To will yourself not to know something specific, you have to have at least a suspicion or an intimation of what is going on. If not, why would you want to remain ignorant of that particular event or series of events? Wouldn't it be better to face the facts than to give up one's integrity by pretending not to know what one knows in the bottom of one's heart to be the truth?

Nonevaluative knowledge, then, about facts, events, objects, features of the world seems to be good in itself and on account of its consequences. Again, not all items of theoretical knowledge are equally valuable, in general and for oneself. What is clear is that a state of ignorance and error, as such, is simply not choiceworthy; even less so is a communal life that does not value the truth. It would be good to know what our politicians are up to, what next year's wheat crop is going to look like, what happened the night so-and-so was murdered, even if one is not going to act on any of those pieces of knowledge. The public does not always succeed in finding out the truth, but the admission of failure amounts to an affirmation of the value of what has not been attained.

Just as there is individual self-deception, there can be a collective tendency to hide from the truth. There are many examples of a whole people not wanting to know that something is happening in their midst, such as the systematic practice of genocide, torture, discrimination, or domestic violence. A description of the facts would generate a need to take action—which is what people try to avoid.

The reference to self-deception brings us to a new item on our list:

(P.7) Integrity is a basic human good.

What this principle seeks to identify is a complex phenomenon that I am not evaluating now from a moral point of view. By "integrity" I mean the inner harmony of a human being who does not let her thoughts, attitudes, desires, emotions, utterances, and actions go asunder but brings them into fundamental consistency. To say one thing and do something radically different is to be hypocritical; it is to fail to keep the utterance of one's thoughts and the performance of one's actions in mutual harmony. Self-deception also is indicative of lack of integrity because it fails to bring into harmony what one pretends not to know and what one, in a veiled manner, does know.

Integrity, in fact, is the result of bringing the good of practical knowledge to bear on our choices. The mere intellectual realization that it would be good, say, to give up a higher salary in exchange for more time with the family is insufficient if one does not act on it. Practical knowledge, by its very nature, makes immediate claims on our actions, so we would hardly attribute practical wisdom or reasonableness to a person who makes a correct list of things that would be good for her to do but fails to do them.

That integrity is a good is reflected in the fact that we socially blame people for their lack of integrity; at a deeper, personal level, however, it is useful to consider that integrity and inner harmony generate an invaluable sense of self-respect and self-love. People who do not bring their emotions, impulses, and desires in line with their professed convictions (such as alcoholics who want to quit but fail) often end up despising themselves. A life of self-hatred cannot be good, can it?

The social dividends of integrity are not at the same level as the inner good of integrity itself. They are goods nevertheless. The public respect and honor bestowed on people of integrity is fragile because it depends on others' willingness to grant the open recognition it entails. Hence, honor or a blameless reputation is best regarded as a form of confirmation of inner harmony rather than as an independent good.

Some treatments of traditional moral philosophy add a further item to the list of human goods:

Religion is a basic human good.

Moral philosophers who include religion among the items that make a human life a flourishing one usually are following Cicero and many medieval thinkers and hence are invoking a period in the history of philosophy that antedates modern criticism of the assumption that one can prove rationally that God exists.

If God does not exist, then religion—in spite of the benefits of hope in salvation and afterlife or the uplifting joys of communal worship—would be an illusory good. At its very heart there would be a promise of something it cannot deliver. From this belief it is only a short step to the claim that religion in fact is quite detrimental for human beings because it also tends to generate bigotry, intolerance, and certain forms of fanaticism.

On the other hand, if God does exist but there are no satisfactory arguments to prove that, it would still be far from self-evident that religion is a good. Even if it were possible to find such proofs, however, they would take the form of highly complex metaphysical arguments that require advanced philosophical training; thus, their conclusion would hardly be understood by nonspecialists. The goodness of religion, then, would be even more obscure to the layperson than the metaphysical proofs, which would set religion apart from the rest of the goods on our list. Indeed, the expectation for each basic human good was that it would be readily admissible by anyone considering it attentively, without the need or possibility of metaphysical proof.

Someone could claim, of course, that religious faith warrants belief both in the existence of God and in the goodness of religion, but to make this move would be to place the discussion outside the boundaries defined at the outset for moral philosophy. It would be an incursion into theology—a domain of knowledge to whose tenets we cannot request assent from everybody.

We are well advised, then, to take the integrity of human persons as the last item on the list of basic goods that you and I, and anybody else, can accept after a modicum of reflection on their notions and on how they impact on our lives.

Note

1. Aristotle *Nicomachean Ethics* 7–9.

THREE

General Comments on Basic Goods

Chapter 2 submits a list of basic human goods or ultimate goals for human action for your consideration. Chapter 3 does not make additions to the list; instead, it seeks first to clarify how those goods relate to external goods, goods of fortune and human dignity, and more specifically to some goods that have been considered strong competitors for the role of the ultimate human goal (freedom and pleasure). The chapter then returns to the original list to address some general questions it can generate.

External Goods and Goods of Fortune

The goods introduced in chapter 2 are not the only human goods. They are, however, the basic goods—those that are jointly constitutive of an excellent life. On the other hand, we depend on other goods to attain and enjoy the basic ones. Without a certain amount of material things, it is impossible to stay alive, start a family, enjoy beauty, acquire knowledge, and so forth. That is, we need external goods—goods that derive their value from what they allow us to attain. External goods are merely instrumental; they do not possess intrinsic value. Money surely is in this category. Because money has no intrinsic value, it is irrational (i.e., foolish) to make wealth the chief goal of one's life. It also is irrational to use money to acquire things that are bad for us (e.g., drugs or cars that fall apart). Money, then, is neutral and hence can certainly be put to good use.

Among instrumental goods that are internal to a person, it seems appropriate to acknowledge the goods that Greek philosophers called "the goods of fortune": a relatively stable and harmonious family;

a reasonably good physique in terms of beauty and, above all, health; endowment with a certain level of natural intellectual talent, a balanced psychological makeup, and so forth. Although we cannot determine these goods from the start (we can partially modify them as we go along), it is clear that we also require some of these goods to access the basic goods. A person of limited sensitivity will hardly reach a pinnacle of aesthetic enjoyment, a person with a low IQ will not be able to access the more advanced levels of theoretical knowledge, and a psychologically unbalanced person will have trouble making friends. As these examples show, the goods of fortune are not goals. They are the endowment we have at our disposal to set out in pursuit of the good life.

Freedom

There is another kind of good whose location within the constellation of goods is hard to pinpoint. This is the good of freedom.

Freedom functions as a precondition for the enjoyment of most basic goods. Someone who is not legally free cannot enjoy some of the fundamental goods, and the same holds for someone who is severely constrained by a psychopathological condition.

I do not think it is the duty of the writer of a book on ethics to prove that we are free in the metaphysical sense—that is, that the world does not subject us to strict determinism, that our choices are not all forced upon us (perhaps unbeknownst to us) by a chain of antecedent physical causes. The moral philosopher must assume that human beings are free; otherwise her subject matter would vanish. Indeed, the goods that we have been talking about are understood from the start as goods that are achievable by free human agency. How else can we conceive of friendship if not as the result of a free choice to give ourselves to another person and to freely accept affection and commitment in return?

Life, of course, is different. Although we can choose to end it, we cannot freely decide to give ourselves this good in the first place. Life is antecedent to freedom. We have to be alive (and quite some time must have elapsed since our birth) for each of us fully to exercise his or her freedom. In this rather obvious sense, life is more fundamental than freedom.

In modern thought, however, there has been a tendency to view freedom not as the condition that makes possible the enjoyment of goods but as a substitute for them in their role as the ultimate reasons for action. Freedom has been regarded as an ultimate goal, the ultimate good for humans. In its extreme form—aptly labeled "moral libertarianism"—this position seriously challenges much of what is defended in this book; we will return to it in the final chapter.

The view that assigns to individual freedom the place of the ultimate valuable thing probably is the result of a long struggle against horrible restrictions of freedom such as slavery and control of individuals by the omnipotent early modern state. Civil and political freedoms are precious goods, but does that mean that freedom as such is the ultimate human goal? I think not, for a simple reason. What is good for us is not just to choose freely but freely to choose what is good. If we freely choose something that is bad for us, we are better off than if that same option is chosen for us (i.e., if we have to endure or undergo something bad), but we certainly would be better off if we chose freely what is good for us. If this is the case, the evaluation of a choice depends not on whether it was free or not (this is assumed) but on whether something good was chosen. Goods that are not reducible to freedom will be more final than freedom itself.

Hence, freedom is necessary for the pursuit of human flourishing, but it is not a constituent of the good life in the same way the basic goods are.

Dignity

Closely related to freedom is another good that has considerable importance in guiding our actions: human dignity. By "human dignity" I mean the intrinsic worthiness of each and every human being.

The chief problem in discussing this topic is that the word "dignity" in the foregoing sense denotes an intangible property that we seem to possess already. It stands in contrast to goods such as friendship, knowledge, or inner harmony, which we must strive to attain. These are *praktá*, "achievable by human action," as Aristotle would say,[1] whereas dignity is something humans are born with. I would not wish to deny that the statement that persons have an inborn dignity has theological origins, but the claim that human dignity can be trampled upon by certain mean actions on the part of others is intelligible to anyone submitting it to rational consideration.

If the foregoing is correct, dignity does not provide positive reasons to strive to attain it because each individual already is endowed with human dignity. It does provide "negative" reasons for action. It tells us not to do certain things lest we violate the dignity of someone else (or even our own dignity). The overall protection of human dignity, of course, often requires taking positive action and not simply refraining from acting.

When is the dignity of a person trampled upon? Think about a woman who is forced into prostitution by the occupying military forces of the enemy or a Roman slave who is required to attend to every order and whim of his master. What characterizes both cases is that a human being is turned into an instrument for the pleasure or service of someone else. Both individuals doubtless would be better off if they were allowed to live not for the sake of someone else but for their own sakes.

Dignity, in fact, is the attribute of human persons of being ends in themselves, to use a notion defended by the German philosopher Immanuel Kant. Human beings should be respected and allowed to live in pursuit of their own goods. This sense of dignity, of course, does not exclude the possibility that they may grasp the fostering of the ends of others (spouse, children, friends, colleagues, etc.) as an integral part of their own end.

The good of dignity, then, will set a limit to what we may do to human persons, including oneself. To treat a human being as a mere instrument for the attainment of other goals, however laudable, is to violate that person's dignity. To provide sexual favors for the sake of a promotion (or a good grade in a college course) goes against one's own dignity. It shows lack of respect for oneself.

There is a tendency today to regard as a loss of dignity the natural frailties of old age or the use of ugly-looking medical technology to sustain a seriously ill patient. Individuals with Alzheimer's disease or suffering from incontinence, for example, sometimes are treated with disrespect, but this reflects negatively on those who inflict the treatment, not on the dignity of the patients themselves. Likewise, an unscrupulous physician may use excessive life-sustaining technology to forward his own research goals, but this is not necessarily the case. An intravenous line, an oxygen mask, the cables to the machine monitoring the heartbeat, in spite of their unattractive appearance, may well be instruments required to treat a patient with due respect.

In what follows, dignity is understood as a good we ought to respect in our treatment of others and of ourselves.

Pleasure

From the beginning of philosophy, some thinkers have argued that pleasure is *the* natural human goal, and some have defended the view that pleasure is the only thing intrinsically worthy of being desired— other things being desirable only if they lead to pleasure. The thesis that pleasure is the only thing desired for its own sake is called *psychological hedonism,* and the thesis that pleasure is the only thing desirable for its own sake is called *ethical hedonism*. The difference in meaning of the terms "desired" and "desirable" marks the difference between these two doctrines. The former word is used to make descriptive statements, the latter to make evaluative claims. A thing is desirable not only if it can be desired but if it ought to be desired.

Certain modern philosophers, as I have noted, have resurrected ethical hedonism and made it the cornerstone of their conception of ethics by holding that maximization of pleasure for the majority provides the only correct moral standard. According to utilitarianism (the position advocated by Jeremy Bentham and John Stuart Mill), actions are right if they are conducive to the greatest happiness of the greatest number—and by "happiness" they mean pleasure and the absence of pain.

Is this a satisfactory alternative to the views on human goods defended thus far? Is it true that pleasure is the only thing in fact desired for its own sake? Is it the only thing that is desirable for its own sake? Are the basic human goods simply means to attain pleasure? Is their value exhaustively derived from its value?

Fully developed answers to questions about desire and human motivation would require a separate exploration of the many facets of the concept of pleasure—a task for the psychologist or the philosopher of mind that cannot be undertaken here. For our present purposes, let us think of pleasure as a subjective state of consciousness in which a person enjoys herself in one way or another and likes that state of consciousness for itself.[2]

For various reasons, the proposed characterization of pleasure may not be fully satisfactory, but it is sufficient to allow us to raise the following difficulty: Were the first astronomers who sought to measure the distance from the earth to the moon motivated by the expectation of attaining a pleasant state of consciousness or simply by the thought that it would be good to know this feature of the cosmos? Would they have persevered in their search even if they could have anticipated that no pleasant subjective state was bound to ensue?

If you are willing to grant, in this and analogous cases, that people sometimes desire things other than pleasure for their own sakes (in this case, theoretical truth), then you have rejected psychological hedonism. One could retort that those people are ultimately seeking pleasure unbeknownst to themselves, but this objection is unconvincing because it merely blocks the pertinent evidence derived from what people say about why they do certain things. In the absence of independent evidence for the alleged unconscious hedonistic motivation, it seems reasonable to accept that sometimes agents pursue goals other than pleasure. To do otherwise would be to impose on their motives an explanatory pattern derived from the thesis that is itself subject to scrutiny.

Just as psychological hedonism can be rejected by pointing to things other than pleasure desired for their own sakes, likewise ethical hedonism can be rejected by claiming that certain things are valuable in their own right and not only because they are conducive to pleasure. Both a correct and a mistaken calculation of the distance to the moon can produce an enjoyable state of consciousness in the astronomer if the mistake goes undetected, but surely there is value in getting it right and disvalue in being wrong, even if in both cases the subjective feeling is the same. One might object that in the long run, errors in astronomy do not produce a net balance of pleasure over pain for the astronomer, but this attitude is odd. It is unclear how the results of astronomical research should be linked to the subjective states of a particular researcher. It seems far more reasonable to say that errors should be avoided in astronomy simply because there is value in attaining astronomical truth as such. How astronomers feel is not what makes this branch of theoretical knowledge worth pursuing for its own sake. If a theoretical explanation (as opposed to a practical grasp) of the intrinsic good of knowledge is demanded, it should be sought in the deeply embedded, natural human need to know.

Someone might say: I now realize I have to grant that pleasure is not the only intrinsic good, but it is an intrinsic good nevertheless. Shouldn't it therefore be on the list of basic human goods?

Let us consider for a moment a well-known feature of pleasure—or, as many young people say today, "having fun":

> You ask a student what he wants to do this coming weekend, and he replies, "I want to have fun." This is not unexpected, so your next question is, "What are you going to do? Are you going to a party or to the movies?" And he replies, "I don't want to go to a party or to the movies. I just want to have fun." "Do you plan to go hiking or just hang out with friends?" "I have no intention of going hiking or seeing friends or doing anything of that sort. I don't want to do other things. The only thing I want to do is to have fun."

The reason this exchange turns out to be strange is that to have fun or achieve the subjective sensation of pleasure you must do *something*. If your only goal is to have fun, but you don't do anything at all, you won't have any fun. It is an illusion to think that one can aim at pleasure directly, without doing something else or engaging in some activity or other. "Doing" here, as well as "activity," have to be understood in a very wide sense so that they include, for example, seeing someone or even imagining something as *bona fide* instances of these notions.

Sometimes what an agent does can be purely instrumental toward the achievement of pleasure (like the man who gives himself a heroin shot), but pleasure and satisfaction often can be obtained, paradoxically enough, precisely by not seeking the subjective state directly—that is, by doing something perceived as somehow worthwhile in itself, such as engaging in astronomical research.

Pleasure seems to be related to human activity in a very intimate and peculiar way. It is not a detachable consequence of an action, like the salary earned from a week's work, but a concomitant aspect of the action itself—such as the enjoyment one gets from a week of meaningful work. Therefore, the question of whether pleasure is a basic good must be answered by taking into consideration the vast array of actions and activities that generate it.

Judging pleasure and pain in abstraction from whatever generates these subjective states is inadequate. If we abstract from their causes, we would have to say that pleasure is good and worth pursuing and that pain is bad and worth avoiding, making allowance for instrumentally good pains (such as those inflicted by the dentist) and instrumentally bad pleasures (such as enjoying a delicious meal that makes you sick). Indeed, ethical hedonists would argue at this point that what matters is "maximization" of pleasure and "minimization" of pain and that this explains why the instrumental exceptions are not really valid counterexamples. The pain at the hands of the dentist is amply compensated by the greater amount of pleasure derived from being rid of the prior (or potential) pain.

I would suggest, however, that there really are counterexamples to the doctrine that all pleasure is good in spite of the fact that some instances can be instrumentally bad. I would claim, for example, that the intense pleasure of a rapist who takes delight in making his victim suffer is bad—and not simply instrumentally bad. It is a pleasure that is not rational to pursue. Pleasures such as this (assuming that the rapist does not get caught) make a dubious contribution to the maximization of pleasure either of the individual or of the greatest number of individuals. The objection that the amount of pleasure of the criminal is offset by the amount of pain of the victim should be rejected on two grounds: (1) There is really no meaningful way to measure the subjective states of consciousness of different persons to obtain something like a realistic quantitative comparison, and (2) even if a reliable comparison were possible and the amount of pleasure of the rapist turned out to be greater than the amount of pain of the victim, it seems to me that a reasonable observer would still have to reject the claim that the pleasure in question was good.

The example of the uncaught rapist is intended to show that it is a mistake to conclude that pleasure is an intrinsic good by considering it in isolation from its sources. If the sources are taken into consideration, we are led to the conclusion that participation in basic human goods, when grasped as worthwhile and performed in an adequate manner and a suitable context, will be accompanied for the most part by admirable pleasures and deep feelings of satisfaction. Having good friends is an experience that will provoke many enjoyable states of conscience, but it sounds wrongheaded for me to say that I am devoted to my friends for the sake of my pleasant subjective states.

On the other hand, acts of hatred and vengeance also may be accompanied by intense pleasure, but I would not hesitate to dismiss such actions from the list of constituents of a good life. An instance of pleasure, then, is only as good as the activity that generates it; hence, pleasure itself cannot be considered on a par with the basic human goods.

Physical Pain

Within a general treatment of ethical hedonism, a special word should be said about physical pain because it has taken center stage in the present-day discussion of the vexing problems of suicide and euthanasia. Physical pain is a form of suffering that normally accompanies loss of the good of health. It often discharges the positive role of a warning signal and can be said to be instrumentally good. Its counterpart is the diffuse and almost unconscious sensation of well-being that accompanies health. When we are healthy, we go about our daily lives without paying much attention to this feeling, but when we become sick the negative feeling of pain intrudes into our consciousness and hampers our activities. The rational thing to do in these circumstances is to consult a physician, who will probably treat the symptomatic pain and then basically aim at doing away with its cause: the illness itself. The good is being pursued, the bad eliminated.

Unfortunately, certain forms of illness are still incurable. In these cases, the goal of restoring the good of health turns out to be unattainable. Physical pain ceases to have a positive role and remains a permanent witness to the relentless destruction of bodily functions. Pain has become a derivatively bad thing. At this point, the rational thing for the physician to do is to reduce the level of pain and make the patient as comfortable as possible. In accordance with the principle of practical rationality, the derivative bad of pain is thus being avoided.

Physical pain is a dreadful experience, but it is surely not the only one. The loss of any important good is bound to entail suffering. Feeling neglected or abandoned outright by family and friends may be more devastating than the discomfort that can be alleviated by morphine and other means. Health professionals who also provide loving care can make a substantial contribution to the overall condition of their patients.

Rejection of ethical hedonism as developed above is meant to show that pleasure is not the sole and ultimate source of value. The same line of argument should lead us to conclude that physical pain is not the sole and ultimate source of disvalue. Pain is not the ultimate evil for human beings.

Are Basic Human Goods Good without Exception?

Just as we can say that ethical hedonism is false because some pleasures are bad, couldn't we also point to frequent claims that sometimes a specific item on our list may be bad? We have seen that the good of life itself is not compromised by the fact that although life is good for most people, it is not for those who are seriously ill and suffering. We can continue with the rest of the items on our list: health is good in general, although for the young man who is going to be drafted and sent to Vietnam it would be much better to be ill; sometimes it is better not to know than to know; certain friendships are harmful; and so forth. Don't these counterexamples indicate that there is a fatal flaw in the claim that the basic goods provide criteria for goodness because a further, higher principle would be required to decide when a basic human good itself is in fact good and when it is not?

I think it can be shown that these examples do not really entail that the theory must be rejected. What we need is a distinction between an "unqualified" and a "qualified" reflection on a certain notion. By "unqualified reflection" I mean examination of a concept in abstraction or isolation from its different embodiments in the real world. By "qualified examination" I mean the study of a concept that takes into account the circumstances that surround it in a concrete case.

Two analogies illustrate the distinction:

(1) Unqualified examination of a set with two members—or what we may also call "a pair of X's," for any value of X—allows us to know some things in the abstract: that if we add two more X's, we will get four Xs, etc. We also know a few negative things: that insofar as the notion of pair is considered in its full generality, it will be colorless. If we now turn to a pair of (red) apples, we find that (a) some properties are true of the pair of apples by virtue of the fact that it is a pair (e.g., if we add two more apples,

we get four apples) and that (b) some properties are true of the pair by virtue of the fact that they are apples (e.g., their being red).

(2) We all know that water is good for the human organism. This is a general truth that can be explained by biologists who know that water is H_2O and that it plays such and such a role in the human body. Sometimes water is not good for us, however. For example, when we are traveling in certain countries, we are advised not to drink tap water because we might get sick. Application of the distinction to the case of water yields the following result: Examination of water without qualification or reference to particular circumstances tells us what its molecular structure is and why it is good for the organism. Whenever we drink water and it is good for us, it is good by virtue of its being water (not, say, H_2O_2). Reflecting on water in a qualified manner (i.e., in a particular setting) tells us that in certain countries the water purification system is poor and that hence there is a high level of bacteria in the drinking water supply. In such places, drinking water is bad not because it is water but because the water contains dangerous bacteria.

Let us now apply the distinction to the basic goods: Health, we agree, is the good of the body. The fact that there is a war going on and that young, healthy men are going to be drafted and sent to die in a foreign land is not part of the concept of health. It would be better, indeed, for a young man to be ill when the summons arrives, but this does not affect the notion of health. What is bad is not the health of the recruit but the draft and, ultimately, the war. Health by itself, we must admit on reflection, is still a good.

For the sake of brevity, I invite you to repeat this reflection on your own for any of the basic goods to discover where the badness lies. If a friend deceives you, it is surely not because friendship is bad. It is the deception (and the friend's failure to live up to the requirements of friendship) that is bad.

Someone might ask why the strategy of qualified and unqualified consideration was dismissed in the case of pleasure. Couldn't one say that the unqualified consideration of pleasure would show that it is intrinsically good, granting that the qualified consideration might yield bad pleasures (such as those of the rapist)? The reason to reject the application of the distinction to hedonic claims has to do with

GENERAL COMMENTS ON BASIC GOODS 37

the way pleasure is obtained. Whereas you can have health without a draft and water without bacteria, you cannot have pleasure without some kind of activity. Indeed, as we saw, pleasure must be regarded as a concomitant aspect of the action itself. Pleasure, then, should always be evaluated in conjunction with the action that produces it.

Human Goods Are Intelligible Goods

The fact that it is possible to distinguish each basic good itself and its different, often deficient, embodiments reveals a fundamental tenet of the theory: that human goods have a conceptual core that can be intellectually understood. We can conceptually grasp that they are good (and theoretical analysis of the respective notions can explain *why* they are good—a task I do not attempt in this book). Once we have understood and reflected on the core of each of these goods, we can readily distinguish them from the accidental circumstances that lead to the mistaken belief that in certain cases they themselves cease to be good. Recall the analogy with the chemical structure of water and the bacteria floating in it.

From the intelligibility of the core of each basic good (which does not include its embodiments), it also follows that I have no reason to hold that my instantiation of a good is better than yours. Not only would I expect you to deny my dubious claim from the perspective of the original setting for moral philosophy and its egalitarian implications, I also would expect you to argue that there is nothing in the notion of health, for example, that would make mine better than yours and thus justify preferential treatment when we both check into a hospital for the same treatment.

This does not mean that you are equally responsible for your health and for mine. There is very little you can do or say to get me to stop smoking, and even less to get someone in China you have never heard about to quit smoking. Each of us is responsible for the effective pursuit of his or her own goods (and perhaps those of the persons closest to us) because they are activities each person has to choose to participate in. The basic goods are not products that can be given to someone. The idea of "making someone happy"—which suggests giving someone an overwhelming amount of basic goods— is simply irrational. Of course, this conclusion does not rule out the fact that we can and should contribute to the good of others, especially if they are underage or discriminated against or suffering from an unfair distribution of external goods and opportunity. Yet it remains true that the good life can be the achievement only of the person whose life it is.

Basic Goods as Ingredients of the Good Life

The goods enumerated in chapter 2 (life, family, friendship, work and play, beauty, knowledge, and inner harmony) are constituents of good lives or different forms of human fulfillment or happiness. Thus, they provide good reasons to do certain things—on the assumption, of course, that the ultimate good for any rational person is to be happy.

The fact that pleasure is not on the list—either as one item among others or as the one and only item—makes clear that happiness should not be conceived primarily as a subjective state. This is slightly at odds with the ordinary meaning of the English term "happy," which is commonly construed with the verb "to feel." This is not the case for equivalent terms in other languages, however, and we can always resort to expressions such as "human flourishing" or "the good life" to express the notion of an objectively ascertainable, high-quality state for a human being. If we know that a person is alive and well; enjoys affection, love, and family life; has trustworthy friends; has a creative job; and so forth, we can say that she has a good life, regardless of the fact that we cannot get into that person's mind to determine how she feels.

Sometimes, however, people who (from the outside) seem to be leading a good life may report pain and sadness, frustration and hopelessness. In such cases, it is reasonable to conjecture that there is a lack of some good: a lack of physical or mental health, stable relationships, a really fulfilling job, a strong sense of self-love, or something of such ilk. We also could point to our own deprivations. The lesson to be learned is that no human being actually gets to enjoy each and every human good at all times.

Human life is marked by obvious limitations caused by our constitution, our choices, and other accidental factors. The good life is a universal, rational goal that gives direction to large and small decisions by each of us; we should not be surprised, however, if some of the goods remain beyond our reach (e.g., the perfect spouse) or, once possessed, are soon lost (e.g., the deceased spouse). Indeed, we should always be aware of the fact that the inevitability of death entails that at some point in time we will cease to enjoy *any* human good.

Incommensurability and Hierarchy of Goods

The good life is a conceptual ideal (there is nothing of basic value excluded from it), but our lives are far from perfect. Yet we can lead better or worse lives, depending fundamentally on our choices. Is there a fixed hierarchy of goods such that if A is higher than B, and if we always choose A, then our lives will be better than if we choose B? As far as I know, none of the philosophical efforts to set up a fixed hierarchy of basic goods has been successful. Aristotle, for example, argues that excellence in the exercise of theoretical knowledge is the main ingredient in the best life,[3] but it also is clear that in many particular circumstances exclusive pursuit of theoretical knowledge—at the cost, say, of neglecting or harming friends, family, and one's communities—is foolish and wrong. Someone who does that surely is not a good person in the Aristotelian sense of being a virtuous or excellent man.[4]

We often have to choose among competing goods. What we do in such cases is engage in broad prudential comparisons about what goods are more important in general as well as in particular circumstances. It is less important to lose one's job than to lose one's life, but in a given case keeping a risky job to support one's family could be the prudent thing to do.

Prudential weighing of goods according to their importance is quite different, however, from the model of quantitative calculation of goods. Basic goods cannot be reduced to units that it would then make sense to maximize. Are there more units of friendship in having fifty relatively distant friends than in having a few close friends? How many units of work are balanced by how many units of inner harmony? I trust you will agree that the quantitative approach (which is perfectly clear—e.g., for the maximization of yearly profits of a manufacturing company) hardly makes sense for basic human goods.

Even if one grants the Aristotelian doctrine that theoretical knowledge should be valued highly, one can still see that a "lower" good (by comparison) may be the good worth pursuing. In light of my talents (or lack thereof), and given what might follow from a purely theoretical pursuit (I may not find a job as a pure theoretician!), it would be best for me to choose a less glamorous profession.

At times it might seem as if the grounding good—life itself—should *always* take precedence over everything else. Indeed, it is so basic that in most cases it is clear that aiming at other goods at the cost of life would be irrational. Yet there may be circumstances in which not even life should be preserved at all costs. It may be rational to give up one's life (which is not the same as *taking* one's life) so that others may live.

No human good is absolute in the sense that, regardless of circumstances, its pursuit and protection should always and everywhere take precedence over other basic goods. There is no overriding good. Because the order of precedence is not fixed and therefore is far from being obvious to human agents before they face particular choices, we are well advised to develop certain strategies for the pursuit of the human goods.

Notes

1. Aristotle *Nicomachean Ethics* 1.6.1096b33–34.
2. See Brandt (1967), 432–433.
3. Aristotle *Nicomachean Ethics* 10.7–8.1177a12–1179a32.
4. See Aristotle *Nicomachean Ethics* 10.8.1178b5–6.

FOUR

Prudential Guidelines for the Pursuit of Basic Goods

Following a long tradition, I call the ability to identify and successfully pursue what is good for oneself and others "prudence" or "practical wisdom."

There are two reasons why we need prudence or practical wisdom: first, because in the absence of an absolute good or a fixed hierarchy of goods, we cannot automatically decide what it would be best for us to choose in every particular circumstance; second, because the basic goods are formulated in very general terms such that no particular sketch of the good life is valid for everyone. We cannot spontaneously discern which is the best embodiment of the goods for ourselves. The realization, for example, that it would be good to have a job does not tell you which job offer to accept.

The traditional term "prudential"—which we often contrast with "moral"—is apposite at this point because we have not yet crossed the threshold leading into the specifically moral domain. The goods mentioned in preceding chapters are "premoral" goods, so to speak. No moral attributes can be attached directly to them (to be alive or to be sick, as such, is neither morally right nor morally wrong), but morality will be seen to refer back to them.

By its very nature, prudence cannot be reduced to a set of rigid norms; yet the original setting for moral philosophy and the basic principles of practical rationality allow us to justify the guidelines (counsels, precepts) of prudence listed below. Each of them should be understood as filling the gap in the formula "It would be wise for you to exercise . . . in your choices and actions."

Vigilance

Because there is a wide variety of particular goods and nothing that does not have a good aspect to it, it is easy to be misled by an apparent good—by something that may be good and attractive in some respect but turns out not to be really good for a given person at a given point in time, such as the seductive chocolate cake for a diabetic or overtime pay for the workaholic. Vigilance, then, is a prudential attitude of discernment of goods that is necessary because it is irrational (i.e., contrary to the formal principle of practical reason) to choose the apparently good (but in fact, bad, or at least not so good) thing instead of what's really good.

Commitment

Attainment of most basic goods requires considerable effort and dedication. Life teaches us that none of them can be fully attained if they are pursued in a frivolous or casual manner. Staying healthy, raising a family, getting a fulfilling job, becoming a great athlete or artist or scientist or scholar are all goals that demand continuous and sustained sacrifice. The guideline of commitment follows from the realization that, given the importance of the goods at stake, it would be irrational to give up easily in their pursuit. On the other hand, we also realize that we cannot be equally committed to all instances of the goods. It is virtually impossible to excel, say, in athletics, art, science, and scholarship at the same time. It follows that under the guideline of commitment, a certain degree of concentration on certain forms of good is reasonable.

Inclusiveness

The fact that there is a plurality of goods, not just a single good, suggests that it would not be smart to set one's sights on attaining one good to the total exclusion of all others. In such an extreme form of concentration, one would be neglecting the formal principle of practical reason with regard to the other goods.

This does not mean that it would be unwise to have a dominant end in one's life, such as the genuine politician's commitment to the good of the community or the artist's passion for a specific form of art. However, if this passion and devotion entail outright rejection of other goods—if those individuals abandon their families, neglect friends, despise play—then we can say that they are failing to enjoy a vast array of wonderful things. We must conclude that it would be irrational for a person to pursue one basic good at the cost of seriously neglecting the rest.

No one, of course, can go through life focused on one and only one good. The needs of everyday existence force even the most fanatic individual to turn occasionally to goods beyond his or her central passion. The guideline that encourages inclusiveness reinforces this move away from the arbitrary reduction of life to a one-dimensional act and bids us to aim at the broadest possible range of goods. Not to do so is unreasonable.

Detachment

It is reasonable to aim at the widest possible range of goods, but it does not take great insight to realize that we cannot "win them all." Given the obvious limitations of human existence cited in chapter 3, it is clear that there are many goods that a given person will fail to secure for herself. A chronic illness may make physical well-being an elusive goal; the hope of working forever as a professional musician or athlete may be shattered; the expectation of becoming a college professor in theoretical physics simply may not come to pass. The natural obstacles on our way to certain goods are many (poor health, lack of outstanding musical talent, an accident that leaves one with a stiff leg, scarcity of jobs in academia), and more urgent claims on us as human beings often require us to give up certain quests (e.g., the young person who leaves graduate school to support an aging parent).

Coping is the art of doing without certain goods we would like to have but for some factual reason cannot attain. Coping becomes quite difficult, of course, for persons who are obsessed with those unattainable goods. To detach ourselves from the goods that are factually beyond our reach is certainly reasonable. It also may be reasonable to give up an attainable good for the sake of other goods. Self-denial (but only for a worthwhile good) is not irrational.

To this point I have enumerated purely prudential guidelines or pieces of advice. Failure in vigilance, commitment, inclusiveness, or detachment is not immoral. It is simply foolish in the overall enterprise of living one's life.

Now I add three prudential guidelines that provide the link "downward" to the subset of the prudential that is known as the domain of morality. *A human action ceases to be only imprudent and becomes also immoral when a specifiable instance of a human good is seriously affected (i.e., when there is harm involved).* This can happen through negligent failure to act; a positive, intentional action; or, more generally, unequal treatment.

Impartiality

The guideline of impartiality among persons exhorts us to be practically wise in recognizing that instances of a human good are equally valuable whether they are mine, yours, or someone else's. The value of my life or health is not superior to yours. As I have argued, if I made the claim that it was and detrimental consequences followed for you, you would be entitled to reject my claim within the original setting of moral philosophy, and I would have no argument against you.

Anyone can accept the claim that health is good. As we have seen, however, no one need accept the view that my health is more valuable than the health of others. The former claim is universal, the latter view particular; hence the modern philosophical doctrine that the appropriate test for impartiality is universalizability. A claim that can be granted in principle by any and every interlocutor (actual or potential, male or female, religious or nonreligious, etc.) is thereby impartial. This explains why there need not be a conflict between this guideline and the next one: We can all universally agree that it is rational for a particular mother to give preferential care to her baby. What impartiality rules out is arbitrary preference in the assignment of opportunity, education, jobs, property rights, external goods, or any such contingencies in life because arbitrary discrimination results in harm.

Given the fact that we cannot achieve human goods in isolation from others, the guideline of impartiality or equal treatment of persons (also known as "The Golden Rule") plays such a major role in the communal pursuit of goods that some philosophers have mistaken it for the one and only basic moral norm. Recently, however, many feminist philosophers have argued that the emphasis on impartiality is a mistake that results from male dominance in moral philosophy—a mistake that should be corrected by replacing it by an ethics of care, the specifically feminine moral attitude.

In my view, the main problem with the attempt to ground ethics exclusively on impartiality is that it is a purely formal principle that makes no reference to content (i.e., to things good or bad). In fact, it does not rule out the possibility of a masochist impartially harming each member of a group of people simply because he does not mind being harmed himself. To abandon impartiality altogether, on the other hand, is to do a disservice to women insofar as it provides the criterion to show that women are not being treated fairly. If women are being paid less than men for the same kind of work, we should denounce this differential as a failure in impartiality.

Impartiality (as many feminists agree) should not be replaced, but it should be supplemented by two further guidelines of practical wisdom.

Care

The guideline of care condemns inaction and negligence and tells us that it is irrational not to promote and protect instances of a basic good in oneself and others, individually and in community—specifically when the failure in promotion and protection results in harm. It is irrational not to prevent the loss of an important good or not to try to restore it, if it has been lost. Medicine, in its preventive and healing efforts, is directly under this guideline.

Care, because of its nature, exceeds the domain of what some philosophers call the principle of beneficence (from the Latin expression *bonum facere*): the injunction to perform actions that benefit another. Care also includes benefiting oneself.

It is easy to see that this guideline is grounded on the first part of the formal principle of practical reason ("one ought to do and pursue what is good"), adding to it the further specification that particular goods are to be pursued so that harm (not just inconvenience but deprivation of an important good) will be avoided.

To care for oneself (and others) also requires that one see to it that I (or they) suffer no harm as a consequence of the pursuit of my (or their) good. To care for people is to be alert to their needs, especially those of the weakest among us, and to the way one's actions might affect them. Thus, an imperative of care is to consider the consequences of one's actions.

It should be noted that care embodies many of the concerns of feminist philosophers because it naturally flows from love and friendship and is reinforced by the strong emotions that are concomitant to them. We should care deeply for the goods of those we love. Because those goods are intelligible goods, care should never be guided exclusively by the emotions but always also (and ultimately) by reason. We, men and women, must discern whether true goods are being fostered in an apparent and emotionally charged act of care. Sometimes care will be in conflict with our emotions, as with the nursing student who is asked to give an immunization shot to a terrified child.

Care also accounts for the alleged shortcomings of impartiality as a guide to action. In the exercise of care there is reasonable scope for giving preference to one's spouse, children, closest relatives, friends, and colleagues because one stands in special relations to them, and these relationships generate certain responsibilities. However, if our preference entails serious discrimination and actual deprivation of goods for those who are not close to us, the guideline of impartiality may have been violated.

As we shall see, the guideline of care will provide the grounding for positive moral norms. Because care can take many forms, however, those norms will be less specific and stringent than those grounded on respect.

Respect

The guideline of respect for basic goods holds that it is irrational intentionally to attack or destroy an instance of a basic good (i.e., directly to cause harm). Thus, it is roughly equivalent to what some philosophers call "the principle of nonmaleficence" (from the Latin expression *malum non facere*)—the injunction "Do no evil."

This guideline also is justified by the formal principle insofar as violation of this guideline is the opposite of doing and pursuing goods. The guideline is more specific; the specification that the guideline adds to the principle is the reference to *intentionally caused harm*. It is imprudent not to avoid some food that could make you sick, whereas it is both imprudent and immoral to deliberately poison the food someone is going to eat. In fact, this guideline will be the one that leads to the negative moral norms that are, by their very nature, the most specific and stringent ones—and the ones to be applied impartially.

Unlike care, respect for goods is indeed bound by strict impartiality. Because this guideline tells us that we should never intentionally destroy an instance of a human good because doing so would be an act of practical irrationality, it follows that there is no reason intentionally to harm some persons instead of others or to destroy some goods in preference to others. Recall that this does not hold for care. It may be reasonable to care more for the sick child than for the healthy one, and it may be reasonable to give preference to health over play in certain circumstances, but it is always irrational to attack health—anyone's health.

One might object that "respect" is a term that traditionally is used to identify an attitude due to persons and their dignity, whereas here it is employed in reference to goods. This choice is grounded precisely on the need to provide criteria for the application of the vague notion of respect for persons. Deceiving a spouse, lying to a friend, cheating in a game, or slandering a colleague are failures to respect the dignity of those affected simply because certain goods in which they participate are thereby under attack.

A failure in care may be unintentional, but a genuine failure impartially to respect human goods requires an explicit intention on the part of the agent either to inflict harm or to aim at something that by its very nature entails an attack on a basic good, such as an act of marital infidelity. The reason the person did it may not be to cause harm, but the act—by its very nature—causes harm. This issue raises questions of human agency that we should deal with before we make an attempt to justify the moral norms.

FIVE

Agents, Actions, Consequences

The questions addressed in preceding chapters were normative in nature. Their main purpose was to justify claims about what we as humans ought to do, in the prudential sense of "ought." It would be foolish not to pursue the premoral goods or to neglect the proposed guidelines of prudence.

Before we descend from the prudential to its subset, the moral domain, we should clarify some matters that are not purely normative. A few words about the essential features of human action are required because moral norms, as we shall see, apply primarily to actions. Character—or the habitual disposition of individuals to act in certain ways—also is the subject of moral evaluation, but only derivatively so. We morally praise or blame traits of character (we call them "virtues" and "vices," respectively) that amount to a disposition to perform, on a regular basis, certain kinds of actions.

To morally judge our actions and those of others, we should be able to answer a threefold question:

"Who did what, and why?"[1]

Agents

To ask who did something is to inquire about the agent or the "initiator" of the action (in Aristotle's terminology, its *arché* or "starting point").[2] This is a sensible question because it would be improper, of course, morally to blame a person for something she simply didn't do.

With regard to agency, then, it is important to establish whether a person does or does not directly cause an effect and whether she may be remotely contributing to it. To be clear about these alternatives, let us examine two imaginary cases.

Case One

If Peter hires Paul to kill Mary, and Paul actually kills Mary, Paul is an agent, but Peter also bears causal responsibility because he induced Paul to do it. Mary would not have been killed had Paul not initiated the action, to the performance of which he was hired by Peter. The contract on someone's life is a remote cause of a murder but is not yet murder. Paul may take the money and run (or turn Peter in to the police). The death of Mary is caused remotely by Peter and immediately by Paul. There is a chain of sorts from Peter to Paul and then to the demise of Mary, but the link between Peter and Paul is different from the link between Paul and the death of Mary.

Case Two[3]

Jack, a villain who has kidnapped twenty persons, threatens to kill them all unless Jill, a college student who happens to arrive in the village, kills one of them. If she does, Jack promises to set the other nineteen free.

This sort of example usually generates the following moral question: Wouldn't it be permissible (some would even say obligatory) to kill one person to save the other nineteen? The correct answer, I think, is "No." This may sound bold and perhaps uncaring, but I will try to show that it is the only reasonable answer.

If Jill refuses to kill one hostage and Jack in fact kills all twenty, Jill bears no causal responsibility for their murder because there is no immediate or remote agency linking Jill's refusal and the action initiated by Jack. There is no chain from Jill to Jack and then to the demise of the twenty hostages (like the one from Peter to Paul and then to the death of Mary in Case One). Jill did not do anything to induce Jack or move him to kill the twenty hostages. She did not desire the death of the hostages—in contrast with Peter, who did want Mary to be killed. The causal responsibility now falls exclusively on the shoulders of Jack. Jack—and only Jack—is a murderer.

However, doesn't Jill have to bear something that could be called "negative causal responsibility"? She did not positively encourage Jack to do something, but isn't she somehow responsible for failing to act to prevent Jack's action?

Jill's dilemma can be regarded as follows: Under the guideline of care, the formal principle (FP) tells Jill: "If it is good, do it," and saving nineteen lives is good; under the guideline of respect, however, the FP tells her: "If it is bad, don't do it," and killing an innocent hostage is bad because it destroys a life.

Jill's choice, however, is not a choice between one and nineteen lives—as it would appear at first—but a choice between (a) destroying a life in the expectation that Jack, an independent agent, will refrain from violating the guidance of respect, and (b) sparing a life, in fear that Jack, an independent agent, will violate the guidance of respect. Which agent does what is a crucial consideration.

As an agent, Jill is directly under the guideline of respect. She is only indirectly under the guideline of care because in her case the need to protect goods arises out of the threats and possible future actions of a different agent—who, moreover, could have been joking or could change his mind. Even if it is highly probable (one can never be absolutely sure), however, that the criminally minded agent will take action, Jill still remains bound by respect in what *she* chooses to do.

It seems clear that it would be irrational for Jill—under FP and the guideline of respect—to cave in to Jack's demands. She cannot be held responsible for failing to prevent Jack's seriously immoral action, if it takes place. Again, Jack—and Jack alone—would be a murderer.

From a broader perspective, to assign Jill responsibility for what Jack is bent on doing amounts to granting that one should give in to blackmail whenever the threat is credible and the stakes are high. Whether one's decision is morally right or wrong would then be in the hands of drastically evil agents. The worse they are, the more we should comply with their demands. Surely this situation is intolerable.

As an agent, I should judge primarily the action I myself am going to perform. Nevertheless, some critics might still insist that actions cannot be judged in isolation from their foreseeable or actual results.

Actions

Can an action be judged independently of the further intentions of the agent and of what follows from the action itself? If Jill's intention is to see the hostages released, and if she manages to achieve that, isn't she justified in granting Jack's request?

I think not. Consider a simple example: If I steal your wallet so I can buy some great CDs that have just been released but then change my mind and make a contribution to a soup kitchen for the needy, the fact remains that you have been deprived of some of your instrumental goods. You have been negatively affected, regardless of whether my intended or actual use of your money is good or not. Theft should be judged independently of the further aims of the thief.

An action should be evaluated by how it affects the goods at hand. The key consideration is *the main immediate goal of the action itself.* I am introducing the cumbersome expression "the main immediate goal" to mark a distinction between its referent and (a) the immediate partial goals of an action and (b) the more remote or further goal of the agent. All of these goals, which will be explained as we go along, are targets of human intention.

The main immediate goal of an action is what you attempt to identify to reply to the question: *What is he doing?* Any action involves partial actions in pursuit of partial goals, but we usually can discern what is being done on the whole. If an individual draws a gun and thereby gets someone to hand over her purse, we would say that he engaged in armed robbery. His main immediate goal was to appropriate money that did not belong to him by using or threatening to use violence. That is what he did. If in drawing the gun his main goal was to show it to a potential buyer, we would not say that an armed robbery took place. Two very different kinds of action were performed, in spite of the fact that one or more of the partial moves were similar in both cases.

Most philosophers know all too well how difficult it is to give a fully satisfactory analysis of human action, and some have expressed skepticism about even the feasibility of giving a single correct description of an action (e.g., an act of euthanasia, they would claim, could be described equally well as intentionally causing death and as intentionally relieving the patient of her pain). I submit, however, that in ethics we should follow the example of surgeons and the courts.

Surgeons should tell you what kind of surgery they are going to perform on you. Most surgeons start by cutting open the body and thereby achieving a partial goal, but if the main point of the surgery is to remove an appendix, they say they are going to perform an appendectomy; if it is to remove a uterus, they will tell you that you will undergo a hysterectomy. If a doctor offers to perform surgery on you and simply says, "I am going to restore you to health," you should firmly refuse. His remote goal does not tell you what exactly he is going to do to you. He should disclose what I have called his main immediate goal.

Courts of law also have to decide whether a defendant was borrowing money or stealing it, regardless of what his prior moves were and what he meant to use the money for afterward. A patient and a juror cannot afford to be skeptical about the agent's main immediate goal in the performance of an action. Nor can an ordinary person such as you or I be skeptical about our own actions.

Turning once more to the second case under consideration, what would Jill be doing if she gave in to Jack's threats and pulled the trigger? She would be killing a human being, regardless of what Jack may (or may not) do to the rest of the hostages. The outcome of Jack's action would not detract from the fact that the main immediate goal of Jill's action was to deprive one hostage of his life, regardless of her further intentions. To say that Jill was saving the lives of nineteen victims would be an inadequate description of the action because in a different set of circumstances, that same further goal could be achieved, say, by paying ransom to free them, or calling the police, or doing the heroic thing of asking to be killed herself instead of the hostage. In principle, dozens of other things could be done whose main immediate goal is different from the killing of one person.

Actions should be classified as belonging to certain *kinds* by examining their main immediate goal. Identifying the kind of action performed is crucial *because our moral judgments will depend on how human goods are directly affected by each kind of action an agent chooses to perform.*

Yet sometimes it seems that the ends do justify the means—that further motives or expected consequences are the most important factors in the evaluation of an action. There are, indeed, moral theories (aptly labeled "consequentialist theories") that hold that consequences, *and consequences alone*, provide the criterion for morally right and wrong actions.

Consequences

When we are about to do something, we certainly should consider the consequences of our action. If borrowing your roommate's coat (without her explicit consent) will leave her without a warm garment to wear to class on a cold morning, it might be wrong to take it.

Not all consequences, however, are created equal. Standard consequences will be very important for judging the action, but consequences that arise out of a new act on the part of someone else will not. Most of these consequences are out of our hands as agents. The rational thing to do, as we have seen, is to try to prevent bad consequences by means that do not themselves violate the guideline of respect, which applies directly to the action. Care applies only indirectly to Jill under Jack's threat because saving lives is not a standard consequence of shooting people. It is a totally accidental result.

In fact, it is wise to distinguish between accidental and nonaccidental (or standard) consequences of classes of action because the responsibility of an agent will vary accordingly. *A consequence is nonaccidental if it is so linked to the nature of the action that an adequate description of the action would account for it.* A pregnancy, for example, is not a fortuitous or accidental consequence of having sex. A physiologically accurate description of intercourse explains impregnation. That is why a man who unintentionally causes a pregnancy nevertheless is considered responsible and is required to pay child support. No description of the kind of action we call "shooting people" explains, by itself, why some hostages were spared.

Intentions

Our goals are the targets of our intentions. Indeed, a desirable state of affairs becomes a goal for us if we choose to pursue it by effective means (i.e., if we intend it and do not merely wish it). That is why we can say that we intend the partial goals and the main immediate goal of what we do. Nonaccidental consequences may be intended (as in the case of a man who wants to get a woman pregnant) or unintended, but one is not absolved of responsibility for nonaccidental consequences of one's intended actions (as in the foregoing case). Accidental consequences also may or may not be intended; in this type of case, no responsibility can be assigned, especially if those consequences are mediated by the free choices of other people—as in the Jack and Jill example.

Because moral judgment is passed primarily on actions, and actions are specified by intended goals, intentions play a central role in moral philosophy. With regard to consequences, this has led to the well-known problem of the responsibility of an agent for unintended yet foreseeable bad consequences that (in contrast to the Jack and Jill story) *are not mediated by the free choices of a third party.* The analysis has focused on actions that have traditionally been called *causes of double effect.*

Causes of Double Effect

Consider the following examples:[4] There is a bathroom in your home that has two switches. If you want the light on, you flip the switch on the left; if you want the fan on, you flip the switch on the right. You have two causes (the two acts of flipping) and two effects. If you intend both effects, you simply flip both switches.

In the basement, on the other hand, there is a small bathroom in which a single switch turns on both the light and a fan that makes a terrible noise. One cause has two effects. If your intention is to be able to see, you will flip the switch and attain the intended effect of having the light on, but your action will have an unintended side effect: You will have the fan on, making an obnoxious sound. If you could disengage the turning on of the light from the turning on of the fan, you would do so (as you obviously can in the bathroom upstairs); if you can't, however, you simply have to put up with the foreseeable yet unintended consequence of your choice to turn on the light. This does not exclude the possibility that there may be occasions in which you do want the fan on as well. You then intend both effects.

To raise the question, "Why did you do it?" is to try to identify the further goal or intended consequence in the action of an agent. When the action is a cause of double effect, it is perfectly natural to ask: "Did you also intend to produce this second effect, or was it only something you had to tolerate?" Needless to say, the answer cannot always be determined from the outside, even by an attentive observer, because it is an internal decision of the agent. Sometimes almost heroic integrity is required to answer such a question truthfully, even to oneself.

In part because of the difficulty of discerning intentions, the notion of a distinction between intended and unintended consequences has come under attack from different quarters. Much of the discussion focuses on the meaning of the key terms. If "unintentionally" means something close to "unwittingly" or "by chance," it would be odd to say that you turned on the fan (in the basement bathroom) unintentionally. You knew it was going to happen. However, if "unintentionally" means something like "not being the target of your choice," "not being the goal of the act," it is perfectly natural to say that the turning on of the fan was unintentional.

There are similar problems with regard to "wanting." Not wanting to do something (and yet doing it) counts as doing it unintentionally if "not wanting" means "not making it a goal of your act"; on the other hand, it may count as doing it intentionally if "not wanting" simply means "not desiring to do it." We often choose to do (and thus do intentionally) certain things we do not want or desire to do, such as going to a party that we anticipate is going to be quite boring. Conversely, we can desire something we would not choose to cause or bring about intentionally. When he was well advanced in years, the British writer Evelyn Waugh is said to have prayed for death, but he would have been horrified at the prospect of committing suicide. As I have suggested, it is one thing to wish or long for something and a different thing to choose to take effective means to obtain it. Only the latter counts as intentionally doing it.

The foregoing semantic considerations may not resolve all of the puzzles that have been raised by critics concerning actions that can be analyzed as causes of double effect. Nor have we made any application of the analysis to the moral domain. To do so, we will formulate in chapter 6 a normative principle—the Principle of Double Effect (PDE)—that will play an important role in the moral justification of particular kinds of action performed in some tragic cases that closely resemble acts of abortion or euthanasia. That justification, however, can come only after the general question of the moral evaluation of actions has been addressed. By sketching the basics of a theory of action (which is logically independent of the earlier part of the book), this chapter is meant only to prepare the way for that general question.

Let us summarize the results obtained in this chapter. Asking, "Who did what and why?" amounts to (1) identifying the agent who performed the action; (2) determining the main immediate point of the action at hand, which in turn determines the *kind* of action it is (e.g., armed robbery or sale of a weapon); and (3) ascertaining the further intentions of the agent (i.e., the consequences the agent effectively aimed to bring about). Each of us should be blamed or praised for the actions we initiate, for the kinds of action we actually perform, for the intended consequences of our actions, and for their nonaccidental or standard consequences, intended or not. On the other hand, we should not be blamed for what we did not do (and had no way of preventing without direct damage to a basic good), for the unintended consequences of actions that have more than one effect, and for totally accidental consequences of what we did.

How does one go about praising and blaming agents for their actions? That is, how does one pass a moral judgment on a given action?

Notes

1. It often is important to ask about the circumstances surrounding an action. Here, I am ignoring this question to keep the exposition as simple as possible.
2. Aristotle *Nicomachean Ethics* 6.2.1139b5.
3. Adapted from Smart and Williams (1988), 98.
4. Adapted from Beauchamp and Childress (1994), 209.

SIX

Judging Actions: Moral Norms

The function of moral norms is to guide us in assigning moral predicates to kinds (or species) of actions that are specified by their main immediate goal.

The general norm "For any X, if X is an act of stealing, then X is wrong" states that any act whose main point is to appropriate without consent of the owner what does not belong to you is morally unacceptable. By allowing us to classify types of action, norms such as this provide rational guidance in the unavoidable task of morally evaluating our actions and those of others.

Explicit formulation of the norms is important in moral education because they help to instill beliefs and convictions that may become moral knowledge if their justification comes to be properly understood. A human community that did not have an awareness of the moral norms would force its members to face the task of reconstructing on each single occasion the criteria that are required for a correct moral judgment. Needless to say, under such conditions consistency in behavior would be difficult to achieve.

Indeed, aiming at consistent behavior with regard to certain important things, and therefore teaching the moral norms, surely is a practice that is found in any human community because without them it would be impossible to engage in the ongoing enterprise of living together. People live together in pursuit of common goals and, ultimately, in the pursuit of basic human goods.

It seems, then, that morality is not an optional social arrangement; we cannot do without it because it is crucial for the enhancement and protection of the things that are most cherished by all of us. If this is correct, then *moral norms must be justified by showing that they are grounded on basic goods.*

Moral maturity, in fact, is achieved when a person who has been following moral rules blindly (under social pressure, on the prompting of parents and teachers, or on the authority of religious leaders) begins to understand their rationale. The key is for her to understand that following moral norms is not meant to be an exercise in psychological repression (although for some people norms can become an instrument of neurotic self-destruction) or an arbitrary limitation of one's freedom. On the contrary, it should be understood that these norms provide guidance for applying one's freedom to the successful protection and pursuit of goods—indeed, they often free us from mistakes and obstacles on the way to the good life for ourselves and others.

Norms also are important because they provide justification for our appeals to duty and obligation in everyday life. At colleges and universities, we tell students that they have a duty not to cheat. Why? Because cheating is wrong—because there is a norm that holds that any act of improper acquisition or use of information is impermissible. What does this mean? What kinds of norms are these?

Impermissible Actions

Some norms are negative. They tell us what kinds of actions negatively affect important instances of human goods and therefore are morally wrong. Accordingly, negative norms should be justified by invoking the prudential guideline of respect for goods and then specifying the negatively affected good or goods.

Because negative norms depend on the guideline of respect, as we have seen they should satisfy strict impartiality. If it is morally wrong deliberately to attack an instance of the basic goods of any human person, there is no room for justified preference or discrimination in the infliction of harm.

Permissible Actions

If no basic good is negatively affected, the corresponding action is permissible or OK to do. No norms are needed for permissibility; hence, permissible actions constitute something akin to a default domain: If no norm states that an action is either impermissible or obligatory, it follows that it is permissible.

Obligatory Actions

Some norms are positive: They tell us what it would be impermissible for us not to do, and they should be justified by appeal to the prudential guideline of care in conjunction with the corresponding good (or goods, if more than one is at stake).

Compared to negative norms, positive norms are less specific. Respect for human life entails that we should refrain from performing one specific kind of action: killing a human being intentionally. Killing can be done in different ways, but the main immediate goal of the action would be the same. Care for life, on the other hand, may entail a host of actions, each having a different main goal—from feeding a baby to funding a good ambulance service for the transportation of accident victims.

Because positive norms are mediated by the guideline of care, they do not require strict impartiality. Some persons, as I have noted, are more directly under our care than others.

Norms

Let us now turn to the norms themselves. I have hitherto used the term "norms" with the implication that there is a unique set of them. This claim, by itself, is highly controversial. Some people would point to the fact that different cultures have different norms, and some philosophers speak as if we could create new norms and make them binding on ourselves.

The reason to think that there is a definite set of norms is their rationale. If norms promote and protect basic goods, and there is a unique set of basic goods that are objective and universal, it is natural to expect that norms form a unique set. If members of a community do not appear to acknowledge a norm protecting a basic good (such as the norm protecting the physical integrity of young women in places where female genital mutilation is practiced), we have reason to criticize that culture for its insensitivity to a dreadful form of harm, and we could add that although the corresponding norm is not presently acknowledged, it exists and it certainly *ought* to be acknowledged.

Introduction of new norms, on the other hand, is fine as long as they are properly justified. Then, however, there is a good chance that they will not be really "new" but merely better or more specific formulations of generally acknowledged norms. There is the further possibility of arguing that the proposed list of basic goods is incomplete (i.e., that one or more items should be added); in this case, we might get norms that have not been generally acknowledged heretofore. I suspect that the development of environmental ethics will lead us in this direction.

In spite of having been recognized in the past, there surely is room for variation in the formulation of each of the moral norms and in the way of setting up the list.

For the sake of consistency with the proposed rationale, my preference has been to present clusters of norms classified under the good primarily affected by the immediate point of the action. We should not forget that, given the complexity of human life, what we do often affects more than one good and that therefore the corresponding norm could be classified under different headings. Lying to a friend is an attack on knowledge and on friendship. Thus, the classification presented here is not unalterable. It represents one way of reaching some degree of clarity about things that are important to know when choosing and acting.

Because the aim of this book is to provide only a broad outline of the foundations of "our common morality," I introduce the moral norms in their most general form. I make few attempts to resolve questions of casuistry or particular application to hard cases. Such inquiries should come *after* the general norms have been formulated and justified. Moreover, the following exposition does not claim to be exhaustive. A comprehensive treatment would have to include at least norms for sexual ethics and private property.

(R.1) Norms Concerning Human Life

Life is so basic that the moral command "Do not kill" (i.e., the norm forbidding the intentional killing of a fellow human being or oneself), can be regarded rightly as fundamental in moral thought.

From this norm it appears to follow at first sight that abortion, infanticide, murder, suicide, and active euthanasia, as well as the death penalty, killing in warfare, and self-defense, are all morally wrong actions. Some of these kinds of action have become highly controversial; I address two of them (abortion and euthanasia) in separate chapters.

Much of the debate centers on the question of whether a given case falls under the norm. If a fetus is not a human being, abortion does not fall under the norm; neither does self-defense, if the killing is not intentional. One also might claim that there are justifiable exceptions to the norm. If the good of the community requires the execution of a criminal, the death penalty would be a justifiable exception; likewise, if one's country is attacked, killing in its defense also would be permissible. The key point, however, is that all parties to the debate acknowledge, implicitly or explicitly, that *there is a norm to the effect that one should not intentionally kill people.* Any deviation from the norm calls for painstaking justification.

Because I do not deal with capital punishment or war in this book, I simply mention here that the traditional acceptance of these forms of killing is related to the fact that the norm has been understood as a prohibition against killing *innocent* human beings. A criminal and an aggressor would fall outside the scope of the negative norm.

On the positive side are all kinds of actions that entail saving and preserving human lives, directly or indirectly. If you come upon a child drowning in a pool, and you are a good swimmer, you are bound by a norm that requires you to jump in and save the child. Moreover, if you are the lifeguard on duty, you are bound by an even stricter norm to do so: The good to be preserved appears explicitly in the name of your job! On the other hand, if you are at a lake, if the temperature is near freezing, if you are a poor swimmer, if you have had heart problems, it may be heroic for you to jump in, but you are not strictly under the norm that makes it obligatory for you to do so. The reason is that the very same norm bids you to preserve your own life.

The preceding example shows something that will hold for all moral norms: Consideration of the circumstances is crucial for deciding if and when the norm applies. The circumstances must be examined in light of the generic goods at stake, however. Refusal to jump in to avoid ruining your new outfit obviously will not do.

The good of health was mentioned in close connection with the good of life, and most general norms relating to it are easy to discern.

Some of them apply to everyone (such as norms forbidding poisoning of food, polluting of rivers and the environment, selling and doing drugs, excessive smoking and drinking, etc.); some apply more directly to people in the field of health care (doctors, nurses, pharmacists, physical therapists, etc.). Codes of professional ethics have been (and are being) developed in order to explicitly identify their specific obligations.

In this context, an important negative norm should be included that rejects a practice that commonly is used for political purposes and constitutes an attack on health and physical well-being (as well as on human dignity): infliction of torture. Against this norm, consequentialists (and torturers!) in principle could object that torture can be conducive to great benefits for many people. To make their case, they often devise fanciful scenarios such as that a powerful bomb has been hidden in New York City that can be found and defused only by torturing the person who placed the bomb.

I submit that imaginary examples such as this are misleading because they tend to obscure the nature of the act of torture itself and the question of moral responsibility. It is true that there are people bent on doing harm, but prevention of harm should not be purchased at the price of oneself inflicting serious harm in turn.

Thus, the negative norm not to inflict harm takes precedence over the positive one because it is the one that directly applies to the action of the potential torturer. He is morally responsible for his act of torture independently of the moral responsibility of the alleged criminal for his deeds. In fact, in the real world (and ethics is about norms for action in the real world), it usually is unclear whether you are torturing the right person. To determine whether the suspect is guilty or innocent, a judicial inquiry should be conducted; in this case, however, positive incentives (such as plea bargaining) may be more effective than torture—and morally permissible too!

Therefore, it is in perfect consistency with the nonconsequentialist structure of traditional moral thought that the United Nations has declared that freedom from torture should be considered a fundamental human right, not to be violated even when it would seem that torturing one person might prevent serious harm to many.

Just as the guideline of respect grounds the negative norms that forbid killing, harming, and torturing, the guideline of care justifies the moral requirement to protect and promote life, health, and bodily well-being in ourselves and others. This is surely an area of major moral concern.

(R.2) Norms Concerning the Basic Human Community

The best-known traditional moral norm relating primarily to this good is "Do not commit adultery." To appreciate it fully, the defining traits of the family should be called to mind.

The family is a community that arises out of the marriage contract, which in turn determines the institution itself. Here I am employing moral terms, not legal ones; sometimes a contract may be assumed even if no civil (or religious) wedding ceremony has taken place.

If marriage is a contract, it is a particular case of a much broader human practice—that of making mutual agreements, mutual promises, mutual commitments. A brief reflection on our everyday life shows that we live immersed in a thick network of agreements. A college agrees to educate a young person in exchange for a fee, a teacher undertakes to teach for a salary, a student promises to abide by the rules of dorm life, a person makes a commitment to have lunch with a friend, and so forth. It seems clear that agreements generate obligations to abide by them if certain conditions are met, the two most important of which are that the agreement has been freely entered into and that there has been no deception. Coercion and fraud normally make a contract or agreement null and void.

Why do we make contracts in the first place? The rationale for this practice—which at first sight seems to involve the irrational step of giving up one's freedom—is to be sought, as usual, in the human pursuit of goods. Because many goods (certainly the most important ones) cannot be attained in isolation from other people, we see that it is reasonable to make commitments and to accept commitments from others. An individual who shies away from commitments simply will not be able to enjoy certain goods. If you never sign a contract committing you to the purchase of a house, you will never own a house. A person who is "free" from all commitments inevitably will end up empty-handed.

The reference to goods explains why some agreements are more strictly binding than others. Breaking a casual agreement to meet at the cafeteria is not a serious matter, unless there is reason to think your friend will be offended and your friendship might be imperiled.

Marriage surely is one of the most serious commitments a human being can make because of the weight of the goods that depend on people's honoring the commitment: creation of the tightly knit community within which love, friendship, and the transmission of life are key goals. Once children are born, new goals arise; these new goals usually are very demanding—such as raising and educating the young ones.

Traditional moral norms relating to the family are justified by reference to the aforementioned goals or goods. Extramarital sex and infidelity are wrong because actions of those kinds are breaches of a most solemn contract (some cultures even call them "vows") and, accordingly, are a direct attack on the central goods the securing of which is the purpose of the contract. It should come as no surprise to anyone that marriages tend to break down and fail as a consequence of acts of infidelity. These acts usually involve deception, loss of trust and admiration, and, finally, resentment and hatred.

Along this path, other kinds of actions are found that should be firmly rejected under closely connected norms: neglect, abandonment, battery, verbal and physical abuse of spouse, children, or (aging) parents. Marital rape is a particularly heinous attack on the basic human community. On the opposite side, mutual respect, fidelity, love, friendship, and devotion to family members are moral obligations under the guideline of care.

It is interesting to note that some of the aforementioned obligations are contractual (i.e., freely chosen), and some are not. One freely chooses a particular person to be one's spouse (a forced marriage, of course, is an invalid contract), but one does not choose one's parents and siblings. Neither does one choose one's children. One may choose to have children, but not these particular ones (there is plenty of room for surprise here!).

Duties to members of the family other than one's spouse (or adopted children) traditionally have been called "natural" obligations to signal that they are not derived from a freely undertaken commitment. The Latin word for "nature," *natura* (like the corresponding Greek word *physis*) is closely linked to the idea of being born—an act that is not subject to one's choice. I stress the existence of obligations that derive from the fact that one has been born into a given family (which one has not chosen) to show that efforts to provide a purely contractual grounding for moral norms may not be able to account for an important segment of our obligations.

(R.3) Norms Concerning Friendship within Broader Communities

Perhaps the most general negative norm with regard to this all-pervasive good can be conveyed by the injunction "Don't be selfish." Friendships are threatened by lack of generosity—by giving oneself undue preference in the assignment of advantages or the avoidance of discomforts and burdens.

Intimate friendships are harmed by insincerity, hypocrisy, infidelity, and so forth. Less intimate ones, such as business associations, are harmed by breaking of contracts and formal agreements. Attempts to dominate and exercise power over others also are destructive of friendship; so is the use of force. Date rape surely is a serious violation of the good of friendship, especially if the persons involved were more than passing acquaintances.

Norms on the positive side—those bidding us to act with reasonable selflessness—are quite general and hence subject to imaginative deliberation for particular situations. The right answer to the question "How can I advance the good of my friend in the present circumstances?" will vary from person to person and even from day to day. Incidentally, this observation does not open the door to moral relativism (some answers will be definitely wrong); it does show, however, that moral reasoning leaves plenty of room for new and creative developments in the effort to abide by norms whose aim is the flourishing of all kinds of friendship.

Friendship, insofar as it makes of a community a good community, satisfies a fortiori another set of important moral claims: the claims of justice. Friendship is "stronger" (this is what the expression a fortiori implies) in that real friends do not need to worry about treating each other fairly: They do, and do much more than that. When friendship declines or disappears, however, justice acquires special prominence. In a happy marriage, visitation rights make no sense (parents and kids live in the same house); after a divorce, however, a fair and clear settlement of such rights is imperative because the welfare of the children still requires coordination between the estranged parents—and thus generates a community of sorts. Justice is necessary for it to work.

We also are members of larger communities (e.g., a big corporation or a huge country), within which the bonds of affection are very weak or practically impossible. Our moral obligations toward these communities and toward fellow members, therefore, also will entail requirements of justice.

Although justice has made its appearance in our conversation in connection with the good of communities, it seems to be omnipresent in the moral universe. Thus, the norms that govern duties of justice are best treated as pervasive norms after more specific norms have been enumerated—among them norms pertaining to protection of the next set of basic goods.

(R.4) Norms Concerning Work and Play

The most general negative norm with regard to these goods is "Do not cheat." Cheating at work or in play is surely wrong. The game breaks down, and the trust most jobs require thereby is destroyed.

Although the foregoing assertion is true, you will agree, it is highly insufficient. Today, virtually everywhere, the good of work directly intersects with a social mechanism called the free market. This mechanism, in turn, generates new and complex situations that can hardly be judged by means of traditional moral norms.

If having a job is good for an individual, it seems to follow that firing an employee is wrong. Yet we know today that artificially subsidizing jobs that are no longer needed has a cost that also will be borne by other segments of the economy, sometimes in the form of inflation. Hence, it may not be immoral to lay off workers even of a whole sector. Losing one's job is not as serious as losing one's life. A new job can be found, and unemployment benefits can temporarily compensate for the lost good. Conversely, it may be immoral to fire employees if the whole point is to move the jobs to a place abroad where labor laws are seriously defective or simply are not enforced. Sometimes the agents claim that decisions such as these are justified by efficiency within market conditions, but we should not assume that all assignments of goods made through the free market are morally right.

To decide which are right and which are not, philosophers and economists must collaborate in formulating or revising the norms that spell out appropriate and inappropriate behavior in the domain that directly affects the good of work. Some companies and large corporations already have adopted ethics codes with the assistance of specialists in business ethics, and further developments can be expected in this direction. The same can be said of the domain where work and play intersect: professional sports. The need for a code of sports ethics already is being felt.

From the point of view of the individual, the positive norm is that one ought to protect and enhance one's instances of work and play. To run the risk of being fired because of one's carelessness or dereliction of duty would be a violation of the norm. That these requirements of care, especially those relative to play, are not as stringent as the requirements of care with regard to life, health, or physical well-being should be clear by prudential comparison of the goods involved.

(R.5) Norms Concerning Aesthetic Experience

Moral norms within this domain have not been the subject of sustained reflection because of the natural tendency to distinguish between aesthetic and moral values. Artists and poets often claim that their works disclose a dimension that is "beyond good and evil," and they probably are right. Morality, after all, is not the whole story of human existence. A play, a movie, a photograph that defies morality may well be the occasion of a moving and disturbing experience that has a place in a rich and fulfilled human life.

Moral norms in reference to beauty, then, have nothing to do with dictating standards for the production or admissibility of works of art. Among the negative norms are those that ban actions that deprive people of the experience of beauty, such as the wanton destruction of works of art (Hitler's kicking the paintings of the German expressionists would be a good example).

What counts as a genuine instance of artistic beauty is not for moral philosophers to decide; hence, no criteria can be proposed here. That there is beauty in nature, however, and that it makes an important contribution to human well-being should be uncontroversial. Therefore, some of the concerns of the emerging field of ecological ethics should be addressed under this heading. Nature

ought (in the moral sense of "ought") to be preserved not just
because its destruction can have serious negative effects on human
health and physical well-being but also because destroying or im-
poverishing the environment deprives us of the fundamental experience of natural beauty.

(R.6) Norms Concerning Knowledge

The most general norm protecting this good is reflected in the traditional injunction not to lie. The Greek historian Herodotus (fifth
century B.C.) reports that the ancient Persians taught their young three
basic things: to ride, to use the bow, and to speak the truth (*Histories*
1.136). This suggests that they regarded the habit of honesty in
utterance as no less valuable than their two most basic military skills.
The reason is that just as being able to shoot from the saddle was
vital to the defense and expansion of the nation, telling the truth
was regarded as crucial for the internal unity and preservation of
the community.

Lying—expressing in words the contrary of what one thinks with
the intention of deceiving someone who is entitled to know—is destructive of trust and an obstacle in the pursuit of common goals.
Friendships break down and partnerships dissolve if there is habitual
lying on the part of one or more individuals. Sometimes the discovery
of even one instance of lying and deceiving someone else may have
sad consequences.

This confirms the view that our actions may affect more than one
good. Accordingly, the norm against lying also could be classified as
a violation of friendship.

Today we are aware of the fact that there is a deep tendency in
human beings to deceive themselves. We often suspect (or even know)
where the truth lies, yet we may not want to face it because of
otherwise undesirable consequences. People sometimes don't want
to hear about torture being practiced in their country because that
simple admission would force them to take a stand. A deceived spouse
may not want to hear about what she suspects because of the anticipated hardship of living alone, and with less income, after a contested divorce.

Lying to oneself or others can take many forms (e.g., false advertis-
ing, falsifying scientific data, intentionally providing wrong information) and is always an attack on knowledge and truth, either

theoretical or practical. "Do not lie to yourself or others" expresses an important moral norm.

At this point it is common to raise the objection that veracity (i.e., always telling the truth) may have bad consequences—such as the horrible ones that ensue when you tell a Nazi officer that there is a Jewish neighbor hiding in your basement. For a consequentialist, there is an easy solution: Lying is justified, perhaps even obligatory, in a case such as this.

For the human goods tradition and its unwillingness to give up too easily when important values are at stake, there is a genuine perplexity that has generated a complex casuistry involving subtle distinctions such as that between lying and deceiving and between having a right to know and not having it. Strategies of silence, evasion, equivocation, or mental reservation also have been recommended. Deception of the officer by saying, "I saw him walking past the house" (withholding any utterance about the fact that the neighbor then turned around to enter her basement through the back door) would be perfectly permissible as part of an heroic effort to remain faithful to the truth.

The foregoing example of mental reservation (i.e., not revealing the whole truth to someone who is intent on breaking the norm against intentional killing) may sound artificial to many readers. The reason may be the standard technological mentality that judges means exclusively by their effectiveness. The human goods tradition, on the other hand, bids us to ponder how any action affects human goods independently of the further intentions of the agent. The immediate point of mental reservation is not to attack the good of truth but to withhold it from someone who will make a wrong use of it. Practicing mental reservation among intimate friends in matters of importance surely is impermissible.

Fortunately, most readers of this book are unlikely to encounter many Nazis in their lives (in moral philosophy, Nazis are meant to generate a sense of inexorability and firm predictability, which seldom occurs in real life). More common temptations are, for example, lying to a spouse following an act of infidelity or to a patient who has a fatal disease. I argue that cases such as these fall squarely under the general norm against lying. As suggested earlier, knowledge of the truth is an important good for the deceived parties because it allows them freely to react to the new circumstances. Ignorance in such cases restricts their freedom to dissolve or reaffirm a relationship or duly to prepare for death.

The norms of positive care for truth are manifold and perhaps best illustrated by the duties involved in scholarly and scientific research. Among them are duties to be open-minded, to strive for clear thinking, to engage in painstaking research and verification, to admit unfavorable results or unpalatable opinions, and so forth. In a broader setting, it is reasonable to affirm that upholding freedom of speech is a moral obligation under a norm that is grounded on the good of truth.

(R.7) Norms Concerning Integrity

The good of integrity or inner harmony is protected by negative norms that forbid us from engaging in actions that tear us asunder by letting certain passions have the upper hand. Greed—the passion to possess more and more material goods—if catered to, is destructive of inner harmony; so is vanity, the passion to strive for more and more honors and public recognition. Pornography, sexual promiscuity, rape, and so forth also are attacks on the integrity of the perpetrators (as well as the dignity of the victims). The traditional norm forbidding fornication (i.e., sexual activity) outside the setting of marriage and love has its place here.

Integrity has its limitations, however. A person of integrity is someone who acts invariably in accordance with her convictions. Thus, in the examples I have just given I assume an individual who is convinced that action motivated by greed, vanity, or mere sexual desire is wrong. What if an individual lacks these convictions, however, and thinks on the contrary that, for example, indiscriminate sexual activity with competent and willing adults is OK, and acts accordingly? For him there is no lack of harmony between thought and action. The same holds, incidentally, for the Nazi who thinks all Jews should be exterminated. Neither can be accused of hypocrisy or lack of integrity.

These examples show once more that human goods are not absolute goods—that is, beneficial in isolation from all others. Just as the family (or sex) is not really good without love and friendship, likewise integrity without the good of practical knowledge can be seriously detrimental for a given person (and those around her). However, a person who is mistaken about some of the goods, and hence some of the norms, need not be morally blameworthy—as we shall see when we discuss the role of conscience in human action.

Positive norms that protect integrity can be summarized under the norm "Act always in accordance with your convictions," in the understanding that a reasonable person is willing critically to examine those convictions. Restraint and self-control should be natural fruits of the exercise of care for the good of integrity.

(NJ) Norms of Justice

The requirements of justice are present everywhere on the map of morality. The reason, as I have argued, is that, for the most part, basic human goods can be pursued effectively only in community, and justice is required for the adequate functioning of any community—even the community of sorts that is formed by divorced parents. The demands of justice will be vastly exceeded, as we have seen, by the deeds of friendship.

Justice can be approached fruitfully from the perspective of community or from the perspective of the individual. Here we follow the second approach because it best suits our plan of providing a sketch of the good life for persons such as you and me. When we tackle justice from the viewpoint of associations, it is common to start with notions such as that of distributive (or social) justice, discussing early on different principles for fairness in distribution. Indeed, one of the best-known contemporary treatments of this form of justice is identified by the label "justice as fairness."[1] Justice of the individual, on the other hand, appears primarily in everyday language behind the name of a much-valued human quality: honesty (in the sense of "probity" and "uprightness").

An honest person follows the elementary norm of justice encapsulated in the traditional command: "Do not steal." Appropriating an instrumental good that belongs to someone else with no intention of giving it back is a paradigmatic instance of dishonesty that prevents the rightful owner from making use of the item in his own pursuits. Fraud, misappropriation, embezzlement, and so forth are sophisticated forms of stealing, and all are wrong for the same reason: They prevent individuals from enjoying certain goods and thus should be considered attacks on the negatively affected communities. The norms of justice add a further conceptual determination to the norms that ban attacks on communal friendship: They include a reference *not only to other persons but also to what is rightfully due to them.* A person who rightfully owns a car can demand that it be returned to her (after being driven away from the company parking lot) as a duty in justice. This is owed to her by whoever drove it away.

The next step in this direction would be to explain property rights and, more generally, human and legal rights. This explanation, however, is beyond the limits set for this book.

As we move from external goods to the internal good of freedom, we can identify kinds of action that are clearly unjust because they fail to give due respect to this good. Enslavement, kidnapping, coerced prostitution, and so forth are seriously wrong not because they violate property rights but for a deeper reason: They fail to give due respect to human dignity. Respect for their dignity doubtless is the most basic thing we owe to persons, to all persons.

Is every restriction of freedom, therefore, a failure to respect persons? Is there a negative moral norm that prevents individuals or communities from imposing limitations of liberty? Surely not. The reason not to restrict freedom is that individuals need to exercise self-direction in the successful pursuit of the good life. To try to force people to attain a fulfilled existence is simply irrational. In the midst of their pursuits, however, individuals can deprive each other of goods; they can harm each other. Hence, the grounding norm of classical liberalism advocated by Mill and others ("Do not restrict freedom except to prevent someone from harming others") is perfectly sensible from the human goods perspective.

Individuals sometimes can harm themselves, however. Here the classical liberal (and libertarian) reply is, "It's up to them!" Restricting the freedom of an individual for his own good is called "paternalism" and is unwarranted under the liberal norm. Thus, upholders of classical liberalism have to reject certain social policies (e.g., seat belt laws or Social Security contributions) or otherwise find convoluted arguments to show that their deeper-lying rationale is to avoid harm to others. From the human goods perspective, this is unnecessary. If the inconvenience is not significant and the goods at stake are of great weight (life, limb, and income in old age), there is nothing immoral in requiring people to wear seat belts or save for retirement.

Some of these restrictions, of course, may well be ill-advised and unnecessary. If so, they would be unjust. This has to be decided on the basis of a careful consideration of the goods at stake (under the guideline of care), however, not on a blanket rejection of paternalism.

Justice requires us not only to respect free choices (unless they are seriously detrimental to others or to the person herself); it requires us to treat people equally. Arbitrary discrimination on the basis of race, gender, national origin, religious belief, or sexual orientation is unjust. An act of preferential treatment, however, ceases to be arbitrary if there are strong grounds for it. An adequate example would be the preferential hiring of female guards for women's jails to prevent well-documented abuses by male guards. The discrimination in this case is justified because it is grounded on the need to protect the dignity of the inmates. If no instance of a human good is being directly attacked, norms based on the guideline of care can take precedence.

If we now turn our attention from the goods of freedom and dignity to the basic goods achievable by action, it becomes apparent that for the most part, violations of negative norms examined thus far also can be cast as violations of justice, with the exception of the norms protecting integrity. The exception arises from the fact that integrity is primarily a goal for oneself, whereas the notion of justice, as we have seen, includes an essential reference to others.

It should be clear that, in an immediate sense, adultery and cheating, say, also are breaches of justice because they amount to violations of contracts and covenants that explicitly state what is due to the other persons involved. Murder and infliction of physical harm also are unjust because, although they are not strictly violations of contractual obligations, we do owe each other, as a matter of justice, respect for life and health. Because justice requires us to respect other peoples' property (i.e., their tangible and instrumental goods), it much more strongly requires us not to deprive others of goods that, by prudential comparison, appear to be significantly more important than external goods.

It follows from this consideration that cloning a human being would be seriously unjust. Apart from the questionable genetic manipulation involved and the risk of malformations, a cloned person would be deprived *by design* of the elementary good of having a mother and a father—a core ingredient of the family. Note that adopted children are in a different position in that they can seek out their natural parents, in principle—and it is remarkable how often they do so, even when they have loving adoptive parents. There seems to be a deep human need to relate to the persons who transmitted life to us. To manufacture human beings for whom the satisfaction of this need is absolutely impossible surely inflicts serious harm on them.

If respect for the dignity of other human beings, then, is to be explained in terms of due respect for their goods, the norms protecting those goods also will be susceptible of formulation in terms of dignity and justice. Justice, in sum, entails essential reference to others and requires treating equals equally. It also requires treating unequals (in relevant respects) unequally, but in all cases it is the good of others that provides the ultimate reference point for just behavior.

Remarks on Norms

The foregoing norms constitute a catalog of general injunctions that should be accepted by anyone who accepts the list of basic goods and prudential guidelines, especially those of impartial respect and care and, ultimately, the first principle of practical rationality.

Sometimes people speak disparagingly of moral norms, calling them "abstract"—as if they were somehow unconnected to real life and its requirements. Moral norms are, indeed, abstract because they need to be general to provide guidance for large classes of similar cases. "Do not lie" abstracts from differences among particular contemplated lies—and that is precisely how such a command discharges the function of protecting particular instances of truth and trust.

Sometimes people speak as if moral norms restrict freedom. This attitude is highly questionable, however. "Do not commit adultery" does not put an unsurpassable obstacle in the path of a married individual. Its primary function is to convey to him that he would be harming an important good by breaking his promise to be faithful. He can still choose freely either way.

Moral norms provide useful guidance for action, but they do not resolve all moral dilemmas. Many perplexities arise from the fact that, as we have seen, they are general. We often do not know for sure whether a particular kind of action falls under a given norm. Norms require specification—that is, a process of practical thinking that involves consideration of the particular circumstances to see if the norm covers the case at hand. Some philosophers, for example, argue that withholding the truth from someone who does not have a right to know is not lying and hence does not fall under the norm that forbids lying.

Conflicts among Norms

There may be conflicts for an agent who is torn between two conflicting moral demands. Assuming that impartiality is closely connected with respect, the conflicts can be schematically classified as (i) between two requirements of care, (ii) between a requirement of care and a requirement of respect, and (iii) between two requirements of respect.

I submit that (iii) is an empty set because, given the nature of the guideline of respect, negative norms that are based on it cannot conflict. If an individual has an obligation not to kill A and not to physically harm B, both requirements can be fulfilled impartially at the same time simply by not performing the relevant acts (i.e., by taking no action at all).

Care, of course, does require taking action, and that is why there are genuine conflicts of type (i). Sometimes we cannot care for two goods at the same time. In the example involving a child drowning in a pool, we saw that there is no conflict for the lifeguard (she has a clear moral obligation to jump in), whereas there is one for an older gentleman with a heart condition and poor swimming skills. His resolution of the conflict should be based primarily on a consideration of the goods and circumstances (how bad is his heart condition, how deep is the pool, etc.), but neither his decision to jump in (at the risk of his own life) nor his decision not to jump in (to protect his own life) would be morally wrong. Diving in may well be beyond the call of duty ("supererogatory") and even heroic, but failure to act in this case follows the norm of care for one's own life and does not violate any moral norm. If the child, sadly enough, drowns, it will not have been caused by the elderly bystander (unless he pushed that nasty kid into the pool in the first place!).

Some conflicts of care are only apparent, because both goods can be cared for simultaneously. In these cases, once prudence shows that there is no serious danger of harm in one of the alternatives, one would be guilty of neglect if one failed to care for both at once.

Most of the best-known dilemmas discussed in books on ethics are of type (ii)—that is, conflicts that agents face when they are under the claims of respect and care at the same time, as in the Jack and Jill example in chapter 5. When Jill was told to kill the unlucky single hostage, she was under the negative norm that forbids intentional killing, but because that action was supposed to save the rest of the hostages, she was simultaneously under the positive norm that commands saving lives. As we shall presently see, in this and all cases in which violating the guideline of respect amounts to the intentional destruction of an important good, the negative norm takes precedence over the positive one.

The Precedence of Negative Norms

The precedence of negative norms over positive norms in certain circumstances is grounded on the general features of human agency examined in chapter 5. Let us remain focused on Jill, even at the risk of some repetition.

Violation of a negative norm requires that Jill choose to perform an action that directly violates a good. The agent is the cause of the harm.

Violation of a positive norm, on the other hand, requires that Jill fail to act to prevent a harm. The cause of the harm has to be another person (such as Jack) or simply a case of nonhuman agency (such as the drowning of a child who has accidentally slipped and fallen into a pool). If we do not assume that the harm is caused by someone or something else, we are back to the previous alternative—violation of a negative norm.

As we have seen, a person has a direct responsibility for what she intentionally does, not for what others do or what happens accidentally. Any responsibility she might have in the latter cases would be derivative. It would be derived from choices or facts outside her direct control.

Therefore, if the action directly under a person's control falls under a negative norm, she should judge her action by this norm. If it does not fall under a negative norm—that is, if no important good is intentionally under attack in her own action—the action should be judged by any positive norm that may apply. The requirement expressed by the negative norm has to be satisfied first because it is the norm that applies without qualification to the choice of the agent. The positive norm is contingent on what others have chosen. Were it not for Jack's threats, the imperative of care would not arise, whereas the duty not to kill the hostage holds in any case.

Sometimes, however, we have to decide prudentially whether a negative norm takes precedence or not. If the good protected by the negative norm is clearly of lesser importance than the good protected by the positive one, the positive norm may be the one that should guide one's choice. A firefighter trying to reach a person trapped in a building certainly should not follow the norm forbidding the destruction of property. An external good such as a window or a door is not on a par with human life. Because life is the most important good for a human being, and all instances of human life are equally valuable, there is no human good of greater importance that would justify deliberate violation of the negative norm "Do not take innocent human life."

Exceptionless Norms

If certain specific negative norms always take precedence over any positive ones, it becomes apparent that there are at least some exceptionless moral norms (or "absolutes," as they are sometimes, misleadingly, called). Indeed, there is a long tradition—going back at least to the ancient Greek philosophers—that is committed to the view that certain kinds of action are always wrong.

In Plato's *Crito*, Socrates defends the thesis that one should *never* do something unjust to another person. Having been treated unjustly oneself does not justify an exception. Retaliation is wrong because it too is a form of injustice (the corresponding Greek term, *antadikein*, means literally "to treat unjustly in return") and hence falls under the general norm.

Against the Socratic thesis it could be argued that the injunction "never do wrong" is valid universally simply because it is analytically true (i.e., true by virtue of the meaning of the terms). To state that something is wrong or unjust is to state that it is one of the things that should not be done. One still needs a criterion to figure out whether some particular action is just or unjust. If what we do in return for an injustice done to us, for example, is not unjust (under this criterion), it would not be retaliation and hence would not violate the injunction. It would be legitimate punishment. The universality of the norm stands; the key problem for the application of the Socratic thesis becomes judgment about a specific kind of action.

Is it possible to have exceptionless moral norms that are not analytic—that is, that do not include moral terms in the descriptions of the kinds of action that are declared to be right or wrong? Aristotle claimed that adultery, theft, and murder are always wrong and that their names already imply badness.[2] He does not make this claim explicitly in terms of norms, but the claim itself is logically equivalent to a set of three exceptionless norms. Are they analytic? It is not totally clear because Aristotle may mean simply that in his moral community, everyone would agree on the moral wrongness of those actions—a fact reflected in linguistic usage that does not preclude the possibility of describing the same actions without using moral terms. If adultery was defined in Greece as a sexual act involving a married woman with a man who is not her spouse, the claim that adultery is always wrong turns out not to be analytic, even though it does not acknowledge exceptions.

Talk of exceptionless moral norms usually generates uneasiness these days, however. Shouldn't we be more flexible? Isn't it irrational to deny that in special circumstances exceptions should be allowed? Consequentialist philosophers invariably are in favor of exceptions because, as we have seen, they shift their attention from the act itself (and the goods thereby affected) to outcomes, intended or not. They can conjure examples in which, say, marital fidelity leads to undesirable results (think of a variant of the Jack and Jill scenario with Jack now requesting to sleep with Jill, who is married, in exchange for the lives of the hostages) and thus carve an exception to the impermissibility of adultery.

I am convinced that extreme forms of extortion such as this occur only rarely in the real world. Real adultery usually follows an altogether different path. I would insist once again that imaginary examples in which important goods are "maximized" at the price of attacking a single good tend to obscure important aspects of morality. In this case, we may lose sight of the unconditional claim a single basic good may place on us. Indeed, many people in the past and even today report that they experience certain moral claims as unconditional, as an obligation to follow the moral law regardless of consequences—such as the duty of a judge or a jury always to hand down a just verdict, regardless of the riots or political turmoil it may generate.

Exceptionless moral norms are negative and few in number, and their function is to safeguard the most important goods. The sexual intimacy of spouses who have made a lifelong commitment to each other, and thus laid the foundation for a family, is of such value (and is so fragile!) that an exceptionless moral norm for the protection of this good is perfectly reasonable.

A couple can manage to save their marriage after an instance of adultery through forgiveness and reconciliation, but a life taken cannot be reinstated. Therefore, one should be particularly critical of efforts to carve exceptions to a norm that enjoins us to refrain from intentionally taking lives—mine, yours, or that of anybody else.

The Principle of Double Effect (PDE)

Introduction of exceptionless moral rules, however, seems to create a moral quandary of its own by prescribing inaction when something could be done to preserve certain goods. When a child is being attacked or tortured, shouldn't one intervene even at the cost of inflicting harm and, ultimately, death? If one's country is being invaded (with all the ensuing rapes, destruction, and killings on the part of the occupying forces), shouldn't one fight and kill in its defense?

Traditional moral philosophy has struggled with these problems and has come to deal with them by distinguishing sharply between cases in which the intentionally caused harm is instrumental to the good effect (and therefore remain impermissible under the guideline of respect) and cases in which the harm is an unintended side effect of the pursuit of a good.

In chapter 5, in the course of examining the key aspects of human action, we defended the idea that there are causes that can have two effects (such as the switch that turns on a light and a fan) and that it is possible to intend one while not intending the other. The aforementioned claims were descriptive. We now introduce a normative principle that narrows the application of FP, the formal principle of practical rationality, to actions that are indeed causes of double effect.

The PDE may be formulated as follows:

An action that has two effects, one of which is bad, is morally permissible if and only if the following conditions are satisfied:

(1) The action itself is morally permissible—that is, its main immediate goal is neither to attack an instance of a basic human good nor to fail to prevent a harm. The action itself must follow the moral norms.

(2) The intended good effect will not be obtained by means of the bad effect.

(3) The agent does not intend the bad effect. The bad effect should not be a desired and sought goal. It can be foreseen, predicted, or tolerated, but not directly willed.

(4) There will be a favorable proportion or balance (prudentially judged) between the good and bad effects. If the good effect is minimal (e.g., avoiding an inconvenience or protecting an instrumental good) and the bad effect is significant (loss of a basic good), the action is not morally justified.[3]

Several criticisms can be raised against the PDE apart from the objection that all foreseen effects are intended. The light-and-fan example was meant to show that sometimes we simply tolerate consequences of our actions. We do not will them or otherwise choose to pursue them by effective means.

A pertinent objection to the normative principle is that it justifies too much. Couldn't Jill's choice to shoot the unlucky hostage be interpreted as a cause of double effect that accords with the PDE? Doesn't she intend the preservation of the other hostages? Can't the death of the hostage at her mercy be taken as an undesired consequence? I'm afraid not. Although her action could be taken to satisfy condition (4) because human lives are at stake on both sides, her action clearly fails to satisfy the other three conditions. Condition (1) is violated because killing an innocent person is not a permissible kind of action, condition (2) is violated because the death of the hostage is a means to get Jack to desist from his threat, and condition (3) is violated because Jill has to intend the main immediate goal of her own action—otherwise she wouldn't be taking action at all.

As the foregoing example suggests, the conditions that must be fulfilled for a legitimate application of the PDE are so strict that from the other end of the spectrum one could object that the principle justifies too little. This may well be true. The PDE is not a blanket excuse to carve exceptions to the strict protection of the basic human goods. It represents a good-faith effort to affirm the value of the goods protected by exceptionless norms *and* the need to take action in certain extreme cases. Note that consequentialists need not worry about a principle to mediate in such cases because they are committed to the view that, for example, a human life, in suitable expectations of abundant good consequences, may be considered an instrument to be disposed of intentionally. Acceptance of the normative system introduced thus far should lead to firm rejection of such a view.

We turn now to questions of life and death covered by strict negative norms and to possible exceptions to them under the PDE or other considerations.

Notes

1. See Rawls (1971).
2. Aristotle *Nicomachean Ethics* 2.6.1107a9–12.
3. See Fagothey (1976), 32–33; Beauchamp and Childress (1989), 128.

SEVEN

On Abortion

Most readers of this book will never have to make choices on the matters of life and death treated in this chapter and the next, but some will. Many readers, on the other hand, will have to face the issues involved—if not in their own person or that of someone close to them, at least as citizens supporting or rejecting legislation dealing with these practices. Insofar as we are members of a political community, we are all affected by them.

In what follows, no attempt is made to raise the legal and political issues involved in abortion and euthanasia—not because they are irrelevant (they are very important indeed) but because legal and political decisions, in principle, should conform to morality, not the other way around. This does not entail that every sort of immoral action, however trivial, should be made illegal. Experience shows that efforts to impose morality by enacting laws often generate needless repression and injustice. It remains true, however, that morality is independent of (and prior to) what a majority may approve and enact. The majority may be right, of course, but not because of its power or its numbers. It will be right if its decisions are in conformity with practical reason.

There also is a deeper motivation to assign a special chapter to each of these practices. Because they affect the beginning and the end of life, they directly relate to the grounding good; therefore, they are of greater moral import than most other actions we can perform. To remain clear-headed in our judgment in such a controversial domain, we must raise the question of agency (who), the question of the nature of the act itself (what), and the question of motives (why) as we work toward a considered moral judgment.

Who

Since the development of RU-486 pills (mifepristone and miso-prostol), an abortion can be performed by the pregnant woman herself (RU-486) or by a physician who has been trained to perform abortions and does so at the request of a pregnant woman (surgical abortion). An abortion could be performed by a nonphysician and against the will of the woman, but any party to this discussion would agree that such cases clearly are unacceptable and may be set aside. The danger for the woman and the lack of respect for her freedom are obvious.

Direct causal responsibility for the act, then, rests either with the woman herself or with the physician, and remote responsibility rests with anyone (boyfriend, husband, parents, friends, counselor, etc.) who may have encouraged or induced her to make the choice. It is often said that ultimately it should be the woman's free choice and that she should make the decision (though she still needs a willing physician for a surgical abortion or for the prescription of the RU-486 pills). Even granting this point (although it could be argued that the father and the larger community should have a say), however, the fact that the ultimate choice is hers does not make it morally right. Many freely chosen actions are wrong. We must examine the action itself to ascertain whether it is, in fact, right or wrong.

What

What kind of action is an abortion? What is its main immediate goal? In general terms, an abortion is a procedure that a pregnant woman undergoes to interrupt her pregnancy. Men do not undergo abortions, nor do women who are not pregnant.

A pregnancy is the development of a new, biologically human organism in the womb of a woman that starts with the process of impregnation of an ovum (conception) and ends with the birth of a child. There may be philosophical controversies about conception, but a practicing obstetrician trying to determine, say, the age of the fetus or the date when the woman will be due to deliver works with a description of pregnancy like the one just given. Conception and birth are the outer limits of a pregnancy.

How is the interruption achieved? The first of the two RU-486 pills works by relaxing the muscles of the uterus; the second causes contractions that lead ultimately to expulsion of the fetus. In a surgical abortion, the fetus is extracted by the physician by suction or other methods, depending on how advanced the pregnancy is. In both cases, it is fair to say, the direct intention of the action is to terminate a pregnancy by removing the fetus so that there will be no further development and, of course, no birth.

There is no way of avoiding the realization, I'm afraid, that an abortion stops the life of a developing human being before he or she is born. Descriptively speaking, then, an abortion is an act of intentional killing. To this one could object that the primary intention could well be not the death of the child but simply the withdrawal of sustenance. Because the death is a nonaccidental consequence of such withdrawal, however, the causal responsibility still holds, just as it would in the case of ceasing to feed an infant.

Admitting that abortion is a kind of action that is correctly described as intentional killing either directly or as a nonaccidental consequence of an intended action does not tell us whether it is morally justified or not. This is a different question to be addressed after looking at the third descriptive factor.

Why

Any sensitive and compassionate person is bound to realize that there are myriads of reasons why a pregnancy and the ensuing motherhood can be a very heavy burden. A woman may be a teenager for whom having a baby may imply not finishing school and being doomed to low-income jobs; for a more mature woman, the pregnancy may threaten career opportunities. A mother already may be overburdened with the care of other children, along with other factors that make her predicament truly oppressive. Indeed, there is a wide spectrum of negative possibilities that range from threat to the life of the mother, at one end, to simply not wanting to face the many inconveniences involved, at the other.

The circumstances of impregnation also are important because this is where the serious responsibility of men comes in. If the pregnancy was a result of rape or incest, or the result of an affair with a married man who is not willing to leave his wife, or came about because the woman gave in to pressure from an irresponsible boyfriend, it may be natural to view the pregnancy as something that is outright bad. (Norms for sexual behavior are determined to a great extent by considerations such as these.) Even in the case of an otherwise happily married woman who already has children, a new pregnancy may generate severe distress, especially if the family's finances are in bad shape. In most of these cases, what a woman intends when she seeks an abortion is the interruption of a pregnancy that appears to be bad for her because it threatens her commendable pursuit of other goods.

The key moral question is whether the positive and fully reasonable pursuit of goods such as education, career, avoiding the birth of a child out of wedlock, the financial well-being of the family, and so forth ever justify an abortion. (I leave for later consideration the case of a threat to the life of the mother.)

The correct reply, given the objective nature of the basic human goods, doubtless is negative. This is one of the cases in which a negative norm takes precedence over positive ones. In other words, the value of a human life (any human life: yours or mine or anybody else's) is so fundamental that it is never permissible to directly attack it, no matter what other goods may be attainable through its destruction. Abortion is a kind of act that falls squarely under the moral norm that forbids intentional killing of innocent human beings.

This reply sounds harsh and insensitive. Aren't there cases in which continuation of a pregnancy would be horrible indeed? To be fully sensitive to such tragic cases, one should exercise one's imagination by putting oneself in the place of both the mother and the child. Thus, we can reflect on the suffering that the woman will be facing (which may turn into joy when she has a smiling girl or boy in her arms or further suffering if the child is given up for adoption—with some comfort, perhaps, from the thought that her child is alive and well); for the child, however, an abortion simply means death—the ultimate bad thing, something neither you, nor I, nor any rational agent would like to have suffered at an earlier stage of one's life. A fetus, of course, is not yet conscious of the loss brought about by death, but it is already the kind of being that will eventually (if all goes well) become what you and I are right now: human beings conscious of the value of our lives.

Summing up, the fundamental argument for the impermissibility of abortion can be cast in the following form:

(Premise 1): An act whose goal is intentionally to attack, harm, or destroy an instance of a basic human good is irrational and morally wrong (the guideline of respect for human goods).

(Premise 2): Life is a basic human good (the first supplementary principle of practical rationality).

(Premise 3): An abortion is an action whose goal is intentionally to attack, harm, and destroy a particular instance of human life (characterization of abortion).

(Conclusion): Abortion is irrational and morally wrong.

The argument seems sound and persuasive. Why, then, do so many people believe that abortion is sometimes—perhaps even always—morally justifiable? Why is it often not regarded as a tragic failure to exercise care for the life of someone else?

I suspect a wide variety of explanations could be offered, ranging from the perceived need to keep abortion available as a contraceptive of last resort to a general cultural insensitivity to the value of life. What really matters for us, though, is what *philosophical* arguments have been given to rationally attempt to show that abortion is indeed permissible. I address two lines of argument that have been prevalent in the scholarly literature and have found many supporters.

"The fetus is not a person."[1]

Like anybody thinking about these matters, upholders of this position accept the principle that it is wrong to kill human beings. "Killing human beings (homicide) is forbidden both by our criminal law and by the moral norms that are accepted in all civilized communities. If the fetus at any point in its development is a human being, then to kill it at that point is homicide, and if done without excuse or mitigation, murder."[2]

Their next step is to deny that a fetus is human in the required sense. In fact, they argue, "human being" can mean two very different things: It can mean (a) "a full-fledged member of the moral community," "a person," and it can mean (b) "a member of the human species," "an individual conceived by human beings." Sense (a) is the moral sense of "human," sense (b) is the genetic sense.

Because the moral norm that forbids homicide applies to persons only (this is taken to be a self-evident moral truth), the key question becomes whether a genetically human fetus is a person or not. To provide a reply to this question, the writers I have in mind take two steps: First, they enumerate criteria central to personhood; second, they ask whether a fetus meets those criteria or not.

The criteria proposed for personhood are consciousness, reasoning, self-motivated activity, capacity to communicate, and self-awareness. Everyone admits that there is some vagueness involved and that something can be a person without having *all* those attributes. What is clear, these writers argue, is that an entity that has *none* of them is not a person. The final step, then, is to observe that a fetus has none of those features; therefore, a fetus is not a person.

Upholders of this view admit that there are some complications arising from the fact that a seven- or eight-month fetus is more *personlike* than a very small embryo, but this is not enough to make abortion impermissible even at a late stage of the pregnancy. As M. A. Warren puts it, "Whether or not it would be *indecent* (whatever that means) for a woman in her seventh month to obtain an abortion just to avoid having to postpone a trip to Europe, it would not, in itself, be *immoral,* and therefore it ought to be permitted."[3]

Is this line of argument correct? Should we accept its conclusion?

An initial difficulty has been pointed out long ago: Given the fact that there is very little difference between an advanced fetus and a newborn infant, the argument also justifies infanticide (i.e., the killing of babies). Some writers have endorsed this conclusion;[4] others have provided separate arguments against infanticide on the basis of the claim that "(t)he minute the infant is born, . . . its preservation no longer violates any of its mother's rights."[5] This reply will not do, of course, because the alleged permissibility of the killing is grounded exclusively on the argument that (i) if a being fails to meet the criteria for personhood, killing it is permissible, and (ii) newborn babies fail to meet these criteria. The rights of the mother (or the interests of anybody else) are logically independent of the invoked premises.

The deeper flaw of the argument is to be found in its claims about personhood. As one of the chief proponents of the view grants, the proposed criteria in fact describe "a normal adult human being."[6] Thus, the argument only allows us validly to reach the trivial conclusion that a fetus is not a normal adult human being.

This, in turn, explains why it has been impossible to answer a question that arises for those who distinguish between being human and being a person. Because they deny that a fetus is initially a person, they must face the question, "When does a fetus become a person?" In other words, when does this decisive change (with its striking moral consequences) take place? Given the true import of the criteria, this question really means, "When does a child become sufficiently adultlike to be considered a person?" There surely is no hope of "drawing the line" during the pregnancy,[7] nor much hope of drawing it later with any degree of precision. This entails that there is no fixed limit to the end of the permissibility of infanticide. The conclusion (as well as any approval of intentional harm to newborns, no matter how young) is enough to warn us that there must be something seriously wrong in the premises from which it was inferred.

Is it really true that we should distinguish the genetic from the moral sense of "human"? Are we really a composite of two radically different ingredients called "genetic humanbeingness" and "person-hood," so that we can, for example, lose one and retain the other? Can this conception of our nature be correct?

I am not worried about the usage of words. In many languages, the words that are equivalent to "human being" and "person" are used interchangeably when referring to people, but I can imagine that calling a small baby or a fetus or an embryo "a person" may sound odd in some linguistic contexts. What really matters is whether there is a set of objective properties that some humans totally lack and persons fully have.

Let us grant that a normal adult has the proposed attributes (they do duty roughly for what philosophers in the past have labeled "freedom and reason"). How are they acquired? Their full exercise doubt-less is the culmination of a lengthy, slow, and continuous process that, as we know today (but Aristotle already suspected), is guided by our genetic makeup. It is because we are humans right from the beginning that we slowly develop into human adults (and not into monkeys or whales).

Many of our capacities develop late in time (and in this sense can be said to be only "potentially" present during the early stages). Human life itself, however, is not potentially, but *actually* there shortly after the sperm and the ovum unite to launch a new, self-developing organism. The basic functions of life (nutrition, growth, reproduction) are fully actualized right from the start. The statement that we do not know when human life begins is falsified by the chapter on fertilization of the ovum in any standard college text on human physiology; it is, of course, an empirical question, not a philosophical (or theological) one.

The standard set of human chromosomes (or deviation therefrom that constitutes a human genetic abnormality) is formed in the process of fertilization. These are the chromosomes that the cells will retain throughout the life of the whole organism and will guide it in its development. Some cells in isolation or an extracted piece of tissue or a few drops of blood will have the same genetic code, of course, as the individual they come from, but they do not constitute a complete organism. They are only parts of a human being.

Once the elementary fact is realized that each of us is an organic whole that retains genetic identity with the embryo (and the fetus and the newborn and the teenager, etc.) we once were, it should strike us as odd that some philosophers talk of persons and fetuses as if they were beings from different planets. Each one of us was a fetus at an early stage of his or her biological career. If we could follow you without interruption in your career in space and time, we would see that you are the same individual as the fetus you were in your mother's womb, but not the same fetus your sister was. There is no spatio-temporal continuity between her career and yours. Each one of us is a unique and irreplaceable temporal being. Although questions of identity are controversial among professional philosophers, elementary claims such as "I was born on such and such a date at such and such a hospital, and then went to such and such elementary school, and then moved to . . ." (i.e., any true claims about my own past) are sustained by the commonsense notion that, although I may have changed in many ways, I am still the same individual I was back then.

Accordingly, if we are biological organisms that retain our identity through time, it is unimportant whether we call ourselves "persons" or "human beings." To this it has been objected that the terms "fetus" and "person" stand in the same relation as "acorn" and "oak tree": An acorn develops into an oak tree, "and it doesn't follow that acorns are oak trees, or that we had better say they are."[8] The difficulty arises, I submit, because the terms "acorn" and "oak tree" describe different stages of the same kind of organism and thus really correspond to "fetus" and "adult" in the case of human beings. Although we do not seem to have a term to cover the whole biological career of an oak organism over time, it is by no means wrong to say that every oak tree is the same organism as the acorn it once was. Every oak tree is, indeed, a biologically successful acorn. Likewise, every adult is a biologically successful fetus.

It also has been objected that irreversibly comatose individuals "*are* human beings but doubtfully qualify as moral persons."[9] A reasonable reply to this view is that in any class of living beings there may be a few defective individuals (i.e., individuals who do not fully exhibit the traits of normal individuals of that class). A dog that has lost a leg, and hence cannot run, is not a normal dog, but it is a dog nevertheless. A patient who has lost some very important human functions is in a defective state, but there is nothing wrong with referring to her as "a comatose person"—with the moral implication that she still deserves respect. This also holds for retarded and otherwise handicapped people. Incapacitation (mental or physical, temporary or permanent, serious or slight) is insufficient to deny personhood. If anything, such individuals should be regarded as weak and vulnerable persons and hence more worthy of our compassion and care than others.

In sum, the claim that a human fetus is not a person is false, and if it sounds offensive to refer to "this tiny entity"[10] as a person, we can say instead "a fetus is a person in his or her earliest stages of development." What matters is not what stage we are going through or what condition we are in at a given moment in time (infancy, adolescence, sleep, incapacitation, full awareness, drowsiness, coma, etc.) but what kind of beings we are. We belong to a biological species whose normal members exhibit some striking features that make us moral agents—that is, agents who are capable of making free choices and demanding respect from each other.

The conclusion that anyone conceived by parents belonging to the human species is a person does not rule out the possibility that there might be other beings, very different from us, who also are persons. In a futuristic, science fiction mode, we can imagine some day coming into contact with Martians or extragalactic individuals who are persons; in a theological vein, we can think of God as a person, as Jews and Muslims do, or even as three persons (as Christians do).

What should be regarded as highly implausible is the view that members of other animal species known to us satisfy any reasonable criteria for personhood—that is, any criteria that manage to spell out what it is for individuals of a certain biological species to be endowed with freedom and reason and thus be responsible moral agents. It seems to be true that dolphins and whales communicate and that chimpanzees show awareness of means/ends connections,[11] but this is a far cry from, among other things, the capacity for abstract thought and the moral (and legal) responsibility we attribute to humans. I hope you will agree with me that taking a dog or a gorilla to court for the sort of misdeeds for which we prosecute our fellow human beings would be silly. It also would be silly to praise a cow for staying in her pasture out of respect for property rights and the moral law. As we stated at the outset—relying on the authority of a prominent animal rights advocate—animals simply are not moral agents.[12]

We should treat animals with due respect, of course, but we should not blind ourselves to the fact that, in spite of the lessons of evolutionary biology, at present a perplexing and wide gap divides humans from other species. It is indeed quite amazing that, as far as our direct empirical evidence goes, we are the only persons around.

To distinguish, then, between the human species and other species at the moment of applying the negative moral norms is something firmly grounded on available, commonsense evidence. To discriminate between individuals within the human species, on the other hand, and to do so on the basis of age (to justify abortion but not infanticide or murder of adults) is arbitrary. If it is morally wrong to deprive a person of her life at age forty, there is no reason why it would be permissible to do so when she is sixty years old, or twenty, or ten, or one, or not yet born, given that she is the same individual. The justification of abortion on the basis of the claim that a human fetus is not yet a person therefore should be rejected.

"Abortion as self-defense."

Some philosophers who otherwise hold that abortion is morally permissible have seen the difficulties facing the view that initially a fetus is not a person.[13] Accordingly, they have searched for arguments that would make some abortions permissible even if it is granted that a fetus is a person. Their position deserves special consideration because it focuses on the conflict of interest between mother and child—a conflict that makes sense only if the full humanity of the mother and the fetus is acknowledged. If a fetus is not a person, there really is no serious conflict of interest, and an abortion becomes a trivial surgical procedure.

In everyday life, conflicts of interest usually are understood by reference to rights, so the abortion debate has also been cast in terms of a conflict of rights. Should the rights of the fetus override the rights of the mother? Can the right to choose override the right to life?

The notion of a legal right is relatively clear. One has a legal right to something if there is a law or a contract granting one the right. For example, foreigners have a right to own property in some countries if those countries have passed laws allowing them ownership, and a person has property rights over her home if there is a legally valid contract granting her ownership of this particular house. The notion of a moral right—a right that is not grounded on positive law or an explicit contract—is a more obscure notion, however, which some philosophers reject. However, it is rights of this latter kind that are at stake when philosophers affirm or deny the right to life of the fetus or the right to choose of the mother. All parties insist that the moral right also should be a legal right.

Although I think that the notion of a moral (or natural or human) right is defensible by reference to basic human goods, I refrain from appealing to it because it would introduce needless complications. It is simpler to focus again on the more fundamental notion of human action. In choosing to do this, I am not departing from the practice of those who accept the argument I am now discussing because their view ultimately rests on some form of the traditional claim that self-defense is a permissible kind of action.

The argument, in essence, runs as follows:

(1) Acts performed in self-defense are morally permissible.
(2) Some abortions are acts of self-defense.
Therefore,
(3) Some abortions are permissible.

There are problems, I think, with both premises of this argument. First, some comments on premise (1). What is an act of self-defense? It is an act in which force is used to stop an aggressor and thus avoid the threat of harm to oneself. Because it aims at the protection of one's goods, especially the good of life, it appears to fall under the guideline of care. The use of force also results in harm to the aggressor, however—even to the point of depriving him of the good of life in the extreme case of killing in self-defense. This is something that seems to violate the guideline of respect. What is clear, then, is that by its very nature, self-defense is a cause of double effect. It is analogous to the bathroom switch that turns on the light and the fan at the same time and therefore falls under the PDE.

The traditional doctrine of self-defense, just like the PDE, is complex and cautious because self-defense can involve many different kinds of situations, with different goods at stake. The doctrine holds that causing harm in self-defense is permissible, but only if some specific conditions are met. There are four such conditions:[14]

(a) The intended goal of the agent in using force must be protection of his goods. If he directly intends harm to the aggressor (because he hates him and wants to use the occasion to get rid of him), his action is morally wrong.
(b) Force may be used only at the time of the aggression itself. Premeditated violence and violent revenge at a later point in time are impermissible. Indeed, they hardly count as self-defense at all.
(c) The use of force is permissible only if there is no other way of stopping the aggression. If persuasion could be effective or the police can be called in, violence should be avoided.
(d) It is impermissible to inflict more harm than is necessary to stop the aggression. This surely is difficult to judge during the confusing moments when the threat is present. The deeper point of this condition is to state unequivocally that self-defense does not justify excessive use of force and certainly is not a license to kill, even unintentionally. If a lesser harm can avert the danger, that lesser harm should be chosen. If there is only a threat to one's purse but not to one's life, killing the mugger would be wrong.

Because these conditions and limitations are roughly accepted by a leading upholder of the self-defense argument,[15] premise (1) may be considered true (under an interpretation that assumes that the four conditions are met) and agreed upon.

The main questions arise with regard to premise (2). Can it be true that an abortion is an act of self-defense? What is certainly false is that *all* abortions are performed in self-defense. Today "the cases are rare in which a pregnancy poses a clear threat to a woman's bodily health"[16]—and without a credible threat to an important good, a defining feature of self-defense is gone. Sympathetic critics[17] have been quick to draw the inference that this realization drastically reduces the number of cases that could be justified by appeal to this argument.

Can *any* case of abortion, then, be an act of self-defense? An initially wanted pregnancy that subsequently becomes unwanted (because the father, say, has walked away) or an unwanted pregnancy caused by contraceptive failure or simply negligence lacks the element of aggression. Thus, the only case left is that of pregnancy resulting from rape. In the case of rape, however, the aggressor surely is not the fetus but the rapist; against him, the use of force—including lethal force, I would hold—is fully justified. Rape is a much more serious offense than theft or robbery.

Even if the fetus could be taken to be an aggressor (which is highly counterintuitive given the fact that an aggressor must initiate an action of some sort), condition (b)—which requires that force be used at the moment of the aggression—would not be met by an abortion, which always takes place some time after the act of aggression (i.e., the rape). It also is doubtful whether condition (a) can be satisfied by a surgical procedure defined by the intended goal of eliminating the fetus itself.

We should conclude, therefore, that no abortion—not even in the case of rape—satisfies the definition of self-defense or the conditions that make it permissible. If abortion in the case of rape cannot be justified as self-defense, is it not justified on some other basis? Isn't an unwanted pregnancy already a heavy enough burden and one resulting from rape a truly unbearable ordeal? I am absolutely convinced that it is, but I once heard that during a discussion of abortion in the case of rape a woman stood up and bluntly said, "My mother was raped," and sat down. I do not know whether the story is true, but it certainly captures the viewpoint of the potential victim. Whether my mother was raped or not, I would much rather be alive today than to have had my life cut short many years ago. I assume the same holds for any rational agent. Childbearing always requires extraordinary generosity and selflessness, and in some cases it can be truly heroic.

Haven't we missed the deeper point involved, however—namely that there are genuine conflicts of interest between mother and child so that sometimes the life of the fetus generates not only suffering and nine months of pain for the mother but also threatens her life? The claims of the grounding good of two human beings are pitted against each other here. As we have seen, such cases today are few and far between; yet they happen. Because it is not the primary aim of this book to solve exceptional and difficult cases but to present the general principles of morality, all I shall do here is invoke the PDE, indicating how it would be morally right to proceed in cases of genuine conflict.

As you recall, the PDE holds that certain actions that have two effects, one good and one bad, are morally permissible if (1) the action itself is permissible, (2) the bad inflicted is not a means to the good effect, (3) the agent does not intend the bad effect, and (4) there is a favorable proportion in the good and bad effects.

A classical application of the PDE has been to justify surgery in the case of a pregnant woman who is suffering from a cancerous uterus. If the tumor continues to grow, her life is threatened; if it is removed together with the uterus, the fetus can no longer live. Surely the conditions for application of the PDE are met (with the possible exception of the third one). The action itself—that is, the hysterectomy whose main immediate goal is the removal of the uterus—is morally permissible in itself. The death of the fetus is not a means to the extirpation of the cancer but a nonstandard consequence of the hysterectomy required for the removal of the tumor. The agent, furthermore, should not intend the death of the fetus. A way of testing intentions here would be to ask if a hysterectomy or an abortion would have been requested had there been no uterine cancer. If the honest reply is "Yes," then both effects were intended. Finally, the goal of preserving the life of the mother is not disproportionate to the loss of the life of the child because both lives are equally valuable.

It can be objected that the PDE could justify any abortion because this form of surgical intervention also is a cause of double effect: It causes the alleviation of a burden for a woman, and it also causes the death of the fetus. Even if we waive consideration of condition (1) so that we do not beg the question, it is clear that the other three conditions are not met. The death of the fetus is the means to the attainment of the good end, not a mere accidental consequence. It is intended because it is the main immediate goal of the procedure or, if not, it surely is the standard consequence thereof. Finally, if anything less than the protection of life is the intended good effect, there will be a significant disproportion between the two consequences of the action.

As we saw, the PDE is a carefully thought-out guideline to face tragic conflicts in a wide range of circumstances where there might be a strong temptation either not to take action at all or, at the other extreme, to treat important goods as mere instruments to achieve other goals. The PDE calls for conscientious fidelity to care and respect. Fortunately, very few pregnancies involve life-and-death conflicts of the sort just mentioned; hence, there seldom is a need to invoke it. The standard moral norm against killing provides adequate guidance in the vast majority of cases.

Returning to our earlier results, we can say that if a fetus is a human being—that is, a person (at an early stage of its development)—and if the moral norm that prohibits the intentional killing of innocent human beings is valid, no directly intended abortion is permissible. The only way to defend the permissibility of abortion is to deny the humanity of the fetus; this, we saw, is untenable.

Further reflection on the goods at stake in the abortion debate actually may lead to a positive view of things. The transmission of life is itself a human good, not the catastrophe or nightmare it sometimes is taken to be in the contemporary debate. Pregnancy is a natural process whose outcome—having a child—is a good that should be judged from the perspective of a broader time frame. The terrible, unwanted pregnancy at age twenty—the one that was going to destroy so many opportunities and prospects (and maybe did)—may end up decades later (and not without much sacrifice) being the beloved child to whom the mother feels so attached. Perhaps that child ends up being the only person the mother can turn to in old age. Even if circumstances require giving up the baby for adoption—a huge sacrifice indeed—the person doing this is following the guidelines of care and respect and thus is a better human being than one who does not.

Notes

1. See Warren (1997). I have this influential article in mind throughout this section.

2. Feinberg and Levenbook (1993), 212.

3. Warren (1997), 140 (emphasis in original).

4. See Tooley (1972).

5. Warren (1997), 141–42.

6. Ibid., 139.

7. Thomson (1997), 123.

8. Ibid., 123.

9. Feinberg and Levenbook (1993), 204.

10. Ibid., 227.

11. Singer (1993), 301–03.

12. Regan (1983) (see page xvi, note 5).

13. Thomson (1997), 123: "I am inclined to agree, however, that the prospects for 'drawing a line' in the development of the fetus look dim. I am inclined to think that we shall probably have to agree that the fetus has already become a human person well before birth. Indeed, it comes as a surprise when one first learns how early in its life it begins to acquire human characteristics. By the tenth week, for example, it already has a face, arms and legs, fingers and toes; it has internal organs, and brain activity is detectable."

14. Fagothey (1976), 219.

15. English (1997), 154.

16. Ibid., 155.

17. Warren (1997), 135.

EIGHT

On Euthanasia

Euthanasia is the ultimate battleground for contemporary moral theories. Abortion often is regarded as a conflict between the life of the fetus and the freedom to choose of the mother—and thus an issue about which upholders of basic human goods and defenders of philosophical liberalism necessarily disagree. If the humanity of the fetus is granted, however, even a strict follower of Mill could agree that abortion is wrong because it entails harm to someone else. No such conflict seems to exist in voluntary euthanasia, however. The life at stake and the freedom exercised are those of the same man or woman. Hence, for a philosophical position that considers freedom to choose an overriding human value, the permissibility of voluntary euthanasia seems to become an indubitable moral truth.

The word "euthanasia" is composed of a Greek adverb and noun that suggest the idea of "dying well" or "good death." What kind of action exactly is euthanasia? As in the case of abortion, the multiple question "Who did what and why?" should help us distinguish euthanasia from other forms of action.

Who

The first issue to consider is whether the agent is the same person who dies or someone else. In the former case, the action is properly labeled "suicide" and is best treated under a separate heading (which, for reasons of space, cannot be attempted in this book). Physician-assisted suicide also should be clearly distinguished from euthanasia because in this case too the main agent is the person who dies. The doctor is expected only to provide the means for the goal intended and attained by the suicidal person.

Euthanasia, then, involves two persons. In principle, any person can be an agent of euthanasia as long as the definition of euthanasia is kept vague, but if it is restricted to terminally ill patients or patients whose pain can no longer be alleviated, it seems that only physicians—or, at least, trained health care providers—can perform acts of euthanasia. Euthanasia that is caused by anybody else would be highly irresponsible, except in very special circumstances. I discuss some of these circumstances below.

What

Euthanasia is an act of intentional killing. If the point of a risky medical procedure, for example, is to remove a tumor and the patient dies, the surgery would not be considered euthanasia. Unintended deaths are not instances of euthanasia.

Nor is euthanasia a matter of simply wishing that the patient die. Euthanasia requires that someone take effective action with the definite purpose of causing the death of a human being.

Active and Passive

It is customary to distinguish between active and passive euthanasia—a distinction that is not strictly equivalent to that between killing and allowing to die. In both active and passive euthanasia, there is an action on the part of an agent, but there is a difference in the primary cause of the death.

If the patient dies because he was given a lethal injection, it clearly is an instance of active euthanasia or killing, and a pathologist performing an autopsy should record it as such. If the patient dies because a respirator was turned off, the primary cause of death reported by the pathologist will be respiratory failure (e.g., from prior acute emphysema). An individual who is not seriously ill may survive after the machine has been turned off. Thus, the turning off of the machine is not strictly the cause of the death of the sick person.

The person turning off the machine may have intended the death of the patient and thus performed an act of euthanasia, albeit an act of passive euthanasia. If the intention of the physician is merely to stop a treatment that is futile and only causes hardship to the patient and her family, however—with death as a foreseeable but not intended outcome—we have a case of allowing to die. This phrase conventionally is taken to signal that the death is not intended, so allowing to die should not be classified as euthanasia at all. This kind of action seems at first sight to satisfy the conditions for the application of the PDE.

The vigorously disputed objection to a justification on the basis of the PDE, of course, is whether it is possible not to intend a consequence that may even be wished. I have argued that in instances of a cause of double effect, it is possible to intend one effect without intending the other, although it is sometimes hard to know whether one also is intending the second effect or not. A test to distinguish passive euthanasia from allowing to die might consist in asking what the doctor would do if, after turning off the machine, the patient continues to live. If he is disappointed and takes further action to end the patient's life, we may infer that her death was intended in the first place.

In the terminology adopted here, then, allowing to die by removing a means that blocks a preexisting fatal condition will be an instance of passive euthanasia only if the death is intended by the agent. Allowing to die is not the same as passive euthanasia and in most cases will be justifiable under the PDE.

Voluntary, Nonvoluntary, and Involuntary

From the perspective of the patient, it also is customary to distinguish three types of euthanasia (any of which may be either passive or active). If the patient freely consents to be killed, the euthanasia is considered *voluntary* or freely chosen. If the patient is incompetent and so cannot give or deny consent, it is *nonvoluntary*. If the patient is competent but does not request or wish to die or if she is incompetent but known not to want to die, the act of euthanasia is *involuntary*.

All parties to the discussion would consider active involuntary euthanasia an instance of murder and thus not subject to philosophical disagreement. Nonvoluntary cases usually are handled by asking empowered relatives to give or withhold consent on behalf of the patient. The envisioned euthanasia then becomes either voluntary or involuntary by proxy. The main moral dispute arises on the issue of voluntary euthanasia (either active or passive). Before we turn to the moral questions, let us examine the third element in the kind of action under consideration.

Why

For there to be a genuine case of euthanasia (or "mercy killing," as it used to be called), the agent must first intend the death of the person; this is the main immediate goal or point of his action. The agent also must have the further goal, however, of relieving a dying person of great suffering. Without this further goal, the action would have to be classified as murder. If a patient is in severe pain but is likely to recover soon or terminally ill but not suffering pain, killing such a patient will hardly count as causing a good death. The alleged mercy is simply misplaced.

In plausible cases of euthanasia, then, there is a conflict that becomes all the more acute if the pain becomes unbearable. Is that sufficient, however, to justify intentional killing? I argue that it is not. Here is the fundamental argument against active euthanasia (voluntary or otherwise):

(Premise 1): Any act whose goal is intentionally to attack, harm, destroy an instance of a basic human good is irrational and morally wrong. (This is the guideline of respect for basic goods under the Formal Principle of practical reason. How seriously wrong the act is will depend on the prudentially determined importance of the good under attack.)

(Premise 2): Life is a basic human good (the first supplementary principle of practical rationality).

(Premise 3): Active euthanasia is an action whose goal is intentionally to take the life of a terminally ill patient to alleviate great pain (definition of active euthanasia).

(Conclusion): Active euthanasia is irrational and morally wrong.

Rejection of passive euthanasia requires a change in premise 3. The goal of the action remains the same, but it is reached not by a direct attack on the life of the victim but by deliberately removing an obstacle that prevents the fatal disease from taking its course. Deliberately halting the chemotherapy of a cancer patient who could recover would be an example.

If the agent does not intend the death of the patient but is moved solely by the aim of removing the burden of a treatment that has become ineffective, the guideline of respect is neither actively nor passively violated; hence, allowing the patient to die could be justifiable. Chemotherapy can be quite excruciating; therefore, it is perfectly rational to stop it once the patient ceases to react positively to it. I leave it to professional bioethicists to further refine the conditions that justify letting a patient die. What ought to be stressed in a book on ethics (of which bioethics is a subset) is the conclusion that acknowledgment of the fundamental value of life does not mandate prolonging the agony and suffering of a hopelessly ill patient. Rejecting euthanasia does not justify actively causing needless pain.

Many philosophers, however, do not accept the foregoing argument. James Rachels—one of the most prominent philosophical advocates of euthanasia—has enlisted the two main trends in recent Anglo-American ethics (utilitarianism and deontology) to show that both types of theory lead to the conclusion that euthanasia is morally permissible.[1]

Utilitarian Argument

Before deploying his utilitarian argument, Rachels quotes a moving report by a journalist describing the suffering of a young man with whom he shared a room at the cancer clinic of the National Institutes of Health (NIH) in Bethesda, Md. The young man was given an analgesic that would work for about two hours; because the physician had prescribed the intravenous shot every four hours, however, the pain would "attack without pity" in the intervals. The young man "would begin to moan, or whimper, as if he didn't want to wake me. Then he would begin to howl like a dog."

The journalist concludes with the reflection that if the young man were a dog he would be taken to the pound and given chloroform to put him to sleep. "No human being with a spark of pity could let a living thing suffer so, to no good end."

The point of the example is clear: Mercy for the young man would justify killing him. The general argument that the case instantiates takes the following form:

(1) Any action is morally right if it increases the amount of happiness in the world or decreases the amount of misery. Conversely, an action is morally wrong if it decreases happiness or increases misery.

(2) Killing a hopelessly ill patient who is suffering great pain, at his request, would decrease the amount of misery in the world.

(3) Therefore, such an action would be morally right.

Utilitarians who also are philosophical liberals immediately sense that there is a difficulty to be faced in the second premise. Why bother to expect a request from the patient? If decreasing overall misery is the justifying principle, it would follow that the patient should be killed even if the "person thinks a miserable life is better than none at all." Freedom here conflicts with utility. Rachels himself calls attention to the problem and thinks it arises because of the "narrow identification of good and evil with happiness and unhappiness" in classical utilitarianism.

Instead of speaking of "maximizing happiness," Rachels introduces the notion of "maximizing interests" and thus produces a new version of the utilitarian argument:

(1) If an action promotes the best interests of everyone concerned, then that action is morally acceptable.

(2) In at least some cases, euthanasia promotes the best interests of everyone concerned.

(3) Therefore, in at least some cases euthanasia is morally acceptable.

This argument, I submit, owes its apparent plausibility to the vagueness of the idea of "maximizing interests." Let's grant that it means something like "doing what is best for someone" and take a look at Rachels' support for the second premise. It consists of a list of effects on people surrounding the young man, had euthanasia been employed in his case:

(i)   It would have been in the young man's best interests because he would have had "an easier death, without additional pain."

(ii) It would have been best for his wife, who was suffering in watching him suffer.

(iii) It would have been in the hospital staff's interest because they could have turned their attention to other patients.

(iv) It would have benefited other patients "since medical resources would no longer have been used in the sad, pointless maintenance" of the young man's life.

(v) If the young man had asked to die (nothing in the journalist's report indicates that he did), his rights would not have been violated.

Note from the start how unconvincing reasons (iii) and (iv) are. Is it necessary for doctors to kill a certain number of their patients to have time to care for other patients? Was the NIH cancer clinic so short of staff? Shouldn't the doctors call for assistance or simply work longer hours? Is this internationally renowned clinic so low on analgesics that precisely those not given to the young man by killing him would go to other patients? I trust that if you, the reader, have ever been to an American hospital or to NIH, you will agree that reasons (iii) and (iv) are so unrealistic that they should be disregarded. No sensible person should think that those are good reasons for killing this particular patient. There are acute problems, of course, relating to the allocation of scarce medical resources on a large scale, and deaths may ensue even from a fair pattern of distribution, but this is different from intentionally killing some patients to give the medicines to others. Those deaths may well be foreseeable, yet unintended.

Reason (v) is meant exclusively to accommodate the element of freedom and is connected to the idea of interests only in the sense that it would not have been in the patient's best interests to be killed against his will. Reason (ii) should make us pause. When there is love and friendship, there may be good reason to spend more time with someone, in spite of the suffering for both persons. Who knows if the wife retains as one of her most precious treasures the memory of a very special exchange of words and holding of hands with her beloved husband that would have been cut short had euthanasia been performed a week earlier? If so, euthanasia would not have been in her best interests. We just don't know. We cannot tell ahead of time. The only remaining reason to be seriously considered is (i).

If it were in the best interests of the patient not to suffer additional pain, why was the young man not given the injection every two hours instead of every four? Indeed, Rachels—in one (though not all) of the several published versions of his views—says literally, "I have discussed this case with some physicians who were indignant that Jack [the young man] was not given larger doses of the pain-killing drug more often."[2] What this moving example demonstrates, then, is that the doctor in charge behaved in a negligent and immoral manner, not that euthanasia would have been justified.

The utilitarian argument for euthanasia has to assume that mercy killing is the *only* alternative to acute pain; in a normal hospital setting, this does not appear to be true.[3] A patient can be sedated. Eliminating pain by death when it can be eliminated by painkillers is analogous to curing a finger wound by amputating the arm. It is a misguided form of action.

Couldn't there be cases, away from a hospital, in which nothing can be done to alleviate the pain? One such case is mentioned in the argument for euthanasia that is based on the Golden Rule, to which we now turn.

Deontological Argument

The term "deontological" is derived from a Greek word that means "what ought to be done" and is meant to convey the idea that a moral agent should do her duty regardless of other considerations. The main idea behind this pattern of moral reasoning is the anti-utilitarian thesis that the morality of an action depends not on its consequences but exclusively on the norm under which it falls. The norm itself is to be accepted or rejected according to whether the agent can will that it be applied universally and impartially—that is, that it also be binding for herself. Any person can will "Do not steal" to be a universal norm because no one wants her property stolen. "Debts should never be forgiven" is a norm that people cannot accept because they would like to preserve the possibility that any future creditors might forgive their debts.

The argument, then, would run roughly as follows:

(1) There is a norm that holds that euthanasia is always impermissible.
(2) No one would want euthanasia to be impermissible in her case if she is the one suffering acute pain.
Therefore,
(3) Everyone would reject the norm that holds that euthanasia is always impermissible.

To support premise (2), we get the same exclusive disjunction that utilitarians assume: Die without pain at the age of eighty or at eighty-plus-a-few days, of a painful affliction that makes you howl like a dog. The possibility of palliative care with effective pain treatment is not even mentioned. Nor is the possibility taken into account of having, during those extra days (or weeks or a month; who knows?), meaningful acts of friendship with one's spouse, children, or friends. Given these possibilities, I for one, would not want euthanasia to cease to be impermissible.

Palliative care again supposes a hospital or hospice setting. What about circumstances in which pain treatment is not available? To illustrate this scenario, Rachels quotes the British philosopher R. M. Hare:

> The driver of a petrol lorry was caught in an accident in which his tanker overturned and immediately caught fire. He himself was trapped in the cab and could not be freed. He therefore besought the bystanders to kill him by hitting him on the head, so that he would not roast to death. I think that somebody did this, but I do not know what happened in the courts afterwards.
>
> Now will you please ask yourselves, as I have many times asked myself, what you wish that men should do to you if you were in the situation of that driver. I cannot believe that anybody who considered the matter seriously, as if he himself were going to be in that situation and had to give instructions as to what rule the bystanders should follow, would say that the rule should be one ruling out euthanasia absolutely.[4]

I also have tried to consider the matter seriously and have reached the opposite conclusion. First, there is the obvious confusion surrounding any accident. It usually is unclear how serious the injuries are. Someone may request euthanasia when in fact he can survive. Furthermore, how would you react to a bystander who starts hitting the victims of an accident on the head instead of trying to do something positive? Wouldn't you have misgivings?

Not wanting to trust my intuitions (moral intuitions are strongly dependent on the way one has been brought up), I have asked a few physicians about this example. The most common reply I have heard is that it is not easy to cause unconsciousness by hitting someone on the head. You have to be very strong; you need an adequate instrument (not any old stick will do); and you have to give an effective blow, or several of them (quite a feat if you are outside a cabin in flames). It doesn't seem to be wise even to attempt it.

The most important point made by physicians I have talked to (and this is the one with general implications), however, is that when armchair philosophers describe scenarios (real or imaginary) that allegedly would justify euthanasia, the more horrible the circumstances depicted (flames, fumes, bleeding wounds, etc.), the greater the chances that the victim will lapse into unconsciousness in minutes, if not in seconds. If the point of euthanasia is to eliminate pain, then in such dire situations it becomes unnecessary. The victim no longer feels anything.

It will seem to you that my objections against the impartiality argument are subjective and grounded at most on informal conversations with unnamed doctors, but given the nature of the argument, that is all that is needed. When Rachels and Hare claim that no one will reject euthanasia for himself at the accident site, you just need one person who rejects it—yourself or someone else—to falsify their claim.

We now turn to a third line of argument that brings euthanasia closest to physician-assisted suicide. These are two kinds of action that, given the difference in agency, should not be confused.

The Argument from Autonomy

If we set aside the question of whether euthanasia contributes to the maximization of general happiness (I honestly do not know whether it does or not because I see no way of measuring happiness in the required sense) and reject the argument that is based on impartiality, it seems that there is a legitimate claim nevertheless in the idea that the wishes of the suffering patient should be honored. Even if the pain may be alleviated, the patient may still want to die—whatever the consequences for general happiness and regardless of what you and I want for ourselves.

This view can be grounded on the so-called principle of respect for autonomy. The word "autonomy" is derived from a term the ancient Greeks applied to any city that was in a position to enact laws (*nomoi*) for itself (*auto*) instead of being under the dictates of a more powerful city. They never applied the term to individuals.

In contemporary philosophy, "autonomy" is used in a variety of ways, but it generally is understood as an attribute of persons who act freely and according to their own plans. By extension, autonomy also is attributed to the actions of individuals if they are not performed under compulsion or external threats and if they are knowingly self-chosen and not chosen by someone else. There are degrees of autonomy, of course; pressure and deception, as well as depression and mental illness—to name only a few factors—can severely diminish the autonomy of certain choices. Ignorance and powerlessness also can reduce the autonomy of individuals, especially their choice of an overall plan.

I am skeptical when philosophers talk about the autonomy of a patient lying flat in a hospital bed. I suspect that no one, not even a physician, can be said to have a plan for his own treatment when hospitalized. He is not in control. He is, in an essential sense, in the hands (and the enormous power) of the medical staff. I think it is more reasonable to say that the patient ought to be free to accept or reject the treatment and procedures that are offered to him. The patient should be free to give or withhold consent to the plan worked out by others. Assigning the label "autonomy" to this freedom to accept or reject proposals framed by someone else sounds to me like an exaggeration.

If there are reasons to doubt that any patient can be really autonomous (in the sense of freely choosing to act according to a self-chosen plan), there are even more powerful reasons to cast doubts on the autonomy of a terminally ill person. She may be depressed and under various forms of psychological pressure, especially if the view that the terminally ill should die and thus stop wasting medical resources (and family assets) becomes socially accepted. I submit that a free choice is unlikely in those circumstances—and a fully autonomous one even less so.

Let us grant, however, that in a rare case there is a perfectly autonomous dying individual who makes the autonomous choice of requesting euthanasia. Does the principle of respect for autonomy justify giving that patient a lethal injection?

In a prestigious book on biomedical ethics, the principle of respect for autonomy is formulated as follows: "Autonomous actions are not to be subjected to controlling constraints by others."[5] In this formulation, the principle is close to the classical liberal principle, omitting the restriction "unless there is harm to others."

The principle operates as follows. Assume two competent adults, A and B. If A makes an autonomous choice, the principle applies to

B and tells her not to interfere with the choice made by A. The principle says that certain actions on the part of B would be morally wrong. Note that the principle does not say anything at all about the morality of the autonomous action chosen by A. The principle offers a moral criterion to judge some actions performed by others, not those of the autonomous agent.

Euthanasia, however, whether active or passive, requires something more on the part of B than simply refraining from interfering with the autonomy (in reality, perhaps, the freedom) of A. It requires B to take action, and about this action the principle also is silent. I submit that what B should do is ask herself what she would be doing and why she would be doing it. The point, of course, is to decide whether doing something as drastic as intentionally killing a patient would be morally permissible (or even required) because the patient requests it. I can imagine that such a request can put enormous pressure on a physician and thus, paradoxically enough, compromise the autonomy of the doctor's own decision vis-à-vis the assumed autonomous patient.

Respect for the autonomy of any person, then, entails not doing certain things. It surely does not logically entail acting on whatever request one receives, even if limited to the private sphere of control of an individual. Because many requests can be quite crazy, a responsible agent should always pause and make an independent judgment about the reasonableness of the request, in light of the human goods and the guidelines of practical reason. An autonomous request, by itself, does not make an act of euthanasia morally permissible.

This might sound rational enough in the abstract, but isn't it cruel not to heed the cry of someone who claims he can no longer endure the pain and the suffering, someone who tells us in tears that he is miserable—that he is leading a wretched life and regards death as a relief and hence as good (for him)? Again, we should pause and let our natural compassion be guided by practical reason. We have to make sure our emotional response leads us to protect goods and reject bad things.

As we saw in chapter 3, what makes a life wretched is not the life itself but the evils endured in that life. First, it is clear that the illness is bad; therefore it is rational for physicians to do what they can to cure the patient. Neglecting a patient is a failure in care and hence morally wrong. When a specific treatment is no longer effective, care demands giving it up, especially if it imposes a painful burden on the patient. Second, physical pain becomes something bad when it ceases to be an early warning of illness and becomes a consequence of progressive physical deterioration. Pain is derivatively bad in that it follows the loss of the basic good of health. It is imperative for physicians to do what they can to alleviate pain. Not to do so is irrational and wrong. In light of the effective means that exist at present, it is impermissible for doctors not to use them in the required degree to diminish the suffering of the patient, even if they unintentionally hasten his death.

However, there is much suffering that is not physical and cannot be alleviated by means of shots and analgesics. It is important to realize that this kind of suffering comes in many forms (loss of a loved one, anxiety about the future, feeling abandoned by one's family and rejected by one's friends, no longer being in control and thus being dependent on the help of others, etc.) and that the man or woman crying out for euthanasia may be suffering in the nonphysical sense.

At this point, the guideline of care reminds us that we human beings have a positive moral duty to provide certain goods to each other, especially to the sick and the dying, which may be classified under the good of friendship. The comfort and affection that certain caregivers provide to the terminally ill satisfy requirements of morality (and of true compassion) that euthanasia does not. Euthanasia is the ultimate failure to care for someone in need.

Slippery-Slope Arguments

No mention has been made of slippery-slope arguments against euthanasia. Some slippery-slope arguments consider the social consequences of accepting a certain practice X that will then lead to practice Y, which in turn would lead to practice Z—an outcome that is unacceptable to all parties to the dispute. In the case of euthanasia, the downward slope takes the following form: If the general prohibition against killing patients is weakened and physicians routinely perform voluntary euthanasia on willing patients, physicians will become desensitized and will soon be practicing nonvoluntary euthanasia with little evidence of what the patients would have wanted for themselves. From that point, there is but a short step to involuntary euthanasia, which everyone considers equivalent to murder.

I take arguments such as this one quite seriously, especially in light of the possibility that this may be happening already in the Netherlands.[6] However, arguments of this nature only help to bring home the negative consequences of the progressive devaluation of life. They play a supporting role, not a central one in rationally deciding the issue. If, by some miraculous arrangement, foolproof safeguards were put in place, and Dutch physicians never practiced nonvoluntary or involuntary euthanasia, it still would be wrong for them to kill a patient at his or her request. Voluntary euthanasia remains an attack on the grounding human good.

Notes

1. Rachels (1986), 151–60.
2. Ibid., 153–54; omitted in Rachels (1993), 46, and Rachels (1999b), 191.
3. See medical literature mentioned in Pellegrino (1998), 270, note 9.
4. Rachels (1986), 159.
5. Beauchamp and Childress (1994), 126.
6. Gomez (1991) attempts to evaluate actual practice in The Netherlands on the basis of available evidence.

NINE

Epilogue: At the Moral Crossroads

Chapters 7 and 8 deal with issues that are vigorously contested today. Any sensitive person, especially any young person, will be torn by the apparent plausibility of the arguments on both sides.

Isn't it true that the already developing child should be given a chance? Isn't it also true that no woman should be forced to have a child she does not want to have? Isn't it true that physicians are supposed to heal, not kill their patients? Isn't it also true that they should be compassionate and actively end the suffering of patients who beg to die?

I have done my best to present the arguments of the most forceful defenders of abortion and euthanasia—and to refute their views. You, the reader, should not take what I say on faith. You should examine not only my discussion but the best writings by others on both sides of these questions. These are accessible and not too long; they are listed in the bibliography. This is what was meant at the outset by the injunction that *we* have to decide in moral matters.

We have to try to find out where the truth lies. The task is not easy. What makes the inquiry especially difficult is that we are dealing with opposing views on matters of principle—matters that therefore cannot be subject to proof from higher premises on which we can previously agree. Nor can we appeal to empirical observation or statistics in our efforts to persuade each other because, as we know by now, moral issues are essentially normative: They are about how we *should* act, not about how people behave in fact. Only factual behavior (not the norm that ought to govern it) is accessible to observation.

The point of presenting an outline of a system of ethics that in my view best represents the mainstream tradition of Western moral philosophy is to show that for centuries, intelligent people have been thinking about these problems in a comprehensive way. Although the claim, for example, that life is good may seem questionable when we consider particular cases of suffering, once you understand it as the cornerstone of a larger whole you also will understand how important it is not to confuse life itself with the evils that we may experience in life—and because of such confusion be tempted to reject one of the foundations of ethics.

The effort rationally to discover where the truth lies in moral issues is a joint effort, but action remains a personal matter. You must make choices, and you should not allow someone else to make them for you. Even if you rely on the authority of your parents, your professors, or your church (which is natural, of course), you must choose whether to accept their authority. If you do not conclude that it is reasonable to assume that their injunctions are correct and their advice is sound, it is irrational simply to obey their directives. Ultimately, you must follow your conscience (as we shall presently see) and be the final judge.

In passing final judgment on the morality of each of your choices, you probably will experience considerable pressure from opposite directions: from the utilitarian mode of thought, on the one hand, and from an exaltation of individual freedom that may be fairly labeled "moral libertarianism" on the other.

Utilitarianism

Utilitarianism weighs heavily on one's decisions because there seems to be something truly compelling in the imperative to maximize happiness. Shouldn't one strive to follow this noble sentiment without further ado? In the biomedical field, for example, shouldn't we strive to find a cure for neurological illnesses that affect thousands of patients and not let research be stopped or delayed by (allegedly) petty claims about the human status of the fetus from which, say, stem cells can be harvested?

Examined closely, the most disturbing ingredients of the utilitarian pattern of thought appear to be its consequentialism and its concept of happiness. By measuring the morality of an action by its consequences, the utilitarian outlook fails to give adequate weight to the fact that important human goods may be trampled in the act itself. Indeed, critics of utilitarianism have been quick to point out that if the end justifies the means, horrible actions may be justified. Stalin may be considered the ultimate utilitarian, if the death of a few million people led to the greatest good of the greatest number of Soviet citizens.

Moreover, because consequences are in the future, there is considerable uncertainty about them. Consequences beget further consequences, and so on. Utilitarians reply that we make all of our decisions on the basis of probable outcomes, not of certainty about them. Surely it is reasonable to make prudential judgments by reference to a probable result ("I will apply for this job because there is some probability I might get it"), but probability is a shaky foundation for moral judgment. "It is permissible for the Air Force to target enemy civilians because then the enemy probably will surrender" is a highly dubious claim. Will the intentional killing of civilians be morally right if the enemy surrenders, and wrong if the enemy does not (assuming in both cases that surrender issues in the greatest happiness for the greatest number)?

To avoid the implication that the principle of utility justifies actions that most reasonable people would consider immoral, some utilitarians have distinguished between act and rule utilitarianism. In *act utilitarianism,* a particular action is justified by reference to the principle of utility ("actions are right insofar as they tend to promote the greatest happiness of the greatest number"); in *rule utilitarianism,* an act is justified by reference to a specific rule that in turn is justified by reference to the principle of utility. In the proposed example, whereas an act utilitarian may approve the targeting of civilians in a particular case, the rule utilitarian might say that the rule that civilians should not be targeted ought to be followed because, in the long run, observing such a rule is conducive to better overall results than giving it up.

Rule utilitarianism comes much closer to common morality than act utilitarianism because the rules it proposes will coincide, for the most part, with moral norms that have been upheld for centuries. Not targeting civilians is part of traditional "just war" theory. An important difference remains, however. The basic utilitarian mode of thought entails that if, in particular circumstances, it can be "clearly foreseen" that intentionally killing a few civilians will vastly maximize utility for the many, it is justifiable to do so. Even according to rule utilitarianism, the rules are not exceptionless; they can always be overruled. The one and only absolute rule is the principle of utility itself.

The position I defend in this book, on the other hand, holds that intentional targeting of civilians is always wrong, no matter what the (alleged) good consequences are. Human goods are willfully being attacked. Of this we are sure. We can add that we are never sure whether overall utility will be maximized, particularly if we take a long-range view of consequences. Perhaps targeting civilians now will induce other armies to do the same in the future, and within a few decades all wars may routinely be conducted with the targeting of civilians. Surely this is a bad outcome. There is, therefore, considerable uncertainty attached even to cases in which the short-range maximization of utility can be "clearly foreseen."

Rule utilitarianism, then, allows for the protection of particular instances of basic human goods (or defense of human rights, if we prefer the language of rights) in the face of claims about the benefits of destroying them. The protection afforded is weak, however, because an exception to the rule is always admissible. Act utilitarianism, on the other hand, has even fewer intellectual barriers standing between its commitment to maximize happiness and the possibility of doing injustice to particular persons.

A leading representative of act utilitarianism, J. J. C. Smart, puts it in striking terms:

Even in my most utilitarian moods, I am not *happy* about this consequence of utilitarianism [that a sheriff in certain circumstances should frame an innocent man to prevent riots that would kill many people]. Nevertheless, however unhappy about it he may be, the utilitarian must admit that he draws the consequence that he might find himself in circumstances where he ought to be unjust.[1]

This is a remarkable statement, for two reasons. First, it betrays the deep uneasiness of the author. He appears to be admitting that his moral conscience does not square with his moral theory. Second, it provides a *reductio ad absurdum* of the theory itself. *Reductio ad absurdum* is a strategy for refuting a theory by showing that it logically leads to something absurd or patently false. In this case, what is absurd is the conclusion that sometimes one ought to do what is unjust.

The conclusion is false because it is a covert contradiction. According to a universally admitted principle of justice (which, as the context shows, Smart implicitly accepts; otherwise he would not feel uneasy), it is always unjust to punish an innocent person. To claim that something is unjust, however, entails that it is something that ought not be done. To claim simultaneously that it ought to be done generates a logical inconsistency. A way out for an act utilitarian would be to give up on the very idea that the demands of justice always ought to be satisfied. This move has unpalatable consequences, however—especially for the innocent victims of injustice. If you and I were in their place, we also would demand that justice be upheld, regardless of consequences.

I submit that the *reductio* strategy will work against any form of consequentialism as long as at least one consequence-independent principle or norm of justice is accepted. And any reasonable person, I think, has to admit some such norm. Wouldn't you admit that it is always wrong and unjust to torture young children, regardless of consequences, even if the consequences include a parent's confession that would prevent harm to many people? Wouldn't you admit that it would always be wrong to punish you if you are innocent? If so, it seems to me that you cannot accept a purely consequentialist moral theory.

Consequences—intended and unintended—should always be considered, of course, but they are not the whole story. *The primary moral question when passing a moral judgment is, how will human goods be affected in the action itself?* Good consequences do not justify an evil deed.

One of the most appealing aspects of utilitarianism has been its emphasis on the greatest good for the greatest number, with each individual receiving equal consideration. As a guideline for public policy, it is doubtless a praiseworthy principle. To build roads where the vast majority of inhabitants of a region will use them instead of building them for the use of a few big landowners doubtless is the right thing to do. Transfer of the greatest happiness principle from the domain of public choice to the heart of the moral domain proves to be troublesome, however.

As we have seen, in the classical version of Bentham and Mill, happiness and value are understood as pleasure and the absence of pain. There have been different attempts to list other items as constitutive of happiness or as additional components of happiness along with pleasure.[2] As the discussion of euthanasia shows, however, physical pain plays such a decisive role in contemporary utilitarian positions that it is fair to say that hedonistic utilitarianism is still a widely shared view. In fact, it could be argued that interpretations of the good as satisfaction of desire or fulfillment of preferences are merely variants of the hedonistic view.

There is a reason why moving away from hedonism is inconvenient for utilitarians. If a list of heterogeneous, nonreducible, intrinsic goods or "interests" is set up, the pervasive quantitative ideas of balance of good over evil, maximization of good, or aggregate or average happiness would all have to be discarded. The project of discovering the value and comparing, say, units of exercise of autonomy against units of deep personal relations sounds to me completely unrealistic.

Let us grant for a moment that feeling pleasure or experiencing happiness at the level of sentience is the common denominator of all forms of the good. Does this mean that the possibility of quantitative measurement required for the application of the principle of utility to concrete decisions thereby has been secured? I think not.

Pleasure and pain are subjective experiences of different individuals that cannot, so to speak, be put side by side to compare them. I can tell you about my toothache, but you cannot feel it. I can tell you that it hurts more than yesterday, but any attempt to prove to you that my tooth hurts more than yours is futile. Any attempt to show that listening to a heavy metal band provides more pleasure than a Mozart piano concerto is bound to be received with skepticism.

Comparisons of pain versus pleasure also are highly doubtful. If a utilitarian man is trying to decide whether to embark on an affair with a woman, can he measure with any degree of assurance the contribution his and her enjoyment will make to the net aggregate of pleasure, subtracting along the way the total units of pain caused to his wife? What are the respective totals of pleasure minus pain that each of his options would cause, taking everyone into account?

Is his decision going to contribute to the greatest happiness of all those who are affected and, ultimately, to the greatest happiness of the greatest number, or is it going to detract from the total happiness?

Some utilitarians have perceived the difficulty.[3] The greatest happiness of the greatest number simply cannot provide workable criteria for the dozens of particular moral judgments one has to pass throughout the day. It is too elusive and remote from the act itself.

The only sensible alternative is to do what human beings have done for centuries: Judge their actions by moral norms that can be justified (and are open to revision) by reference to basic human goods and their particular instances. The aforementioned husband should consider the norm against adultery (and its justification) before proceeding with his affair. Rather than maximize value, he should strive to protect the good that is immediately and directly at stake and avoid the potential bad consequences—not the pain for humanity but the possible breakup of his marriage. This may or may not happen; it is, of course, impossible really to know in advance. Even if there is a high probability that his wife will forgive him, however, her future choice will hardly justify his infidelity.

Particular instances of human goods, then, provide better guidance for moral judgment than utilitarian happiness. Does this mean that the human goods view implies that each person's moral responsibility is to care only for herself and a small circle of friends? Far from it. In traditional moral philosophy, there is a distinctive place for something called "the common good," and many norms (and, therefore, particular moral judgments) are justified by reference to it. The common good, however, is conceived not as the total aggregate of a subjective feeling but as the set of all of those conditions that allow individual persons to pursue their own self-realization (i.e., their participation in objective human goods).[4] Justice is the cornerstone of the common good[5] in the sense that life in community requires that each person be given his or her due in the complex interactions and exchanges that constitute that life. Loss of justice is a harm for the community. Thus, singular acts such as framing an innocent man, discriminating against a person on the basis of race, treating a woman unfairly at the workplace, or oppressing a member of a religious minority are all in themselves (not only because of their consequences) attacks on the common good. All of these claims deserve further development, which cannot be provided here. Let us now turn to a different moral outlook.

Moral Libertarianism

There are several ways of referring to what I have in mind as a force that will continue to weigh heavily on peoples' minds. I adopt the label "moral libertarianism" to describe in rough terms an extreme form of liberalism that obtains when not only the utilitarian concern for the general happiness is abandoned but even particular requirements of care are rejected. A true libertarian sees no moral obligation to save a child drowning in a shallow pool. Neither can he consistently claim a right to help for himself. His sole claim is to be left alone to do as he pleases. This is a recipe for frustration, of course, because it is clear that if each of us is left to his or her own devices there will be many good things that will elude us.

It is not against moral libertarianism, of course, to enter into contracts with other people and thus bind oneself to perform certain actions. The essential condition is that one freely choose to enter into such compacts and undertakings. Thus, contractual obligations are the only moral obligations the libertarian can acknowledge.

Libertarianism is an attractive moral attitude at first sight. It will have no truck with the fantastic claims of utilitarianism that, moreover, entail the potential to severely restrict freedom and submit minorities to the whims of the majority. There is something admirable—almost worthy of Prometheus, the titan who defied the Greek gods—in moral libertarianism's rejection of any imposition on the part of others.

Can the libertarian mode of thought, however, make a substantial contribution to one's particular moral decisions? Just as utilitarianism is unrealistic in its invitation to base moral decisions on broad future expectations that are really unknowable and unmeasurable, likewise libertarianism is unrealistic in its assumptions about the context of human action.

Freedom, of course, is distinctively human, but it cannot account for everything we are or have. We did not freely choose to be conceived and be born, we did not choose the family that nurtured us, nor did we freely select our parents and siblings (or lack thereof). We may have freely chosen a friend or a spouse, but the fact that we initially came into contact with this specific person (and not hundreds of others) was not chosen. We did not initially choose the broader communities (the linguistic community, the social class, the political community, etc.) of which we are a part. And so on. The point I am trying to bring across is that, although because of our freedom we can affect and change much in our lives, there is a "substratum" that is plainly given. Important noncontractual obligations arise from that substratum. We have duties, for example, to parents and siblings we never selected. The fact that we have noncontractual obligations toward other human beings (i.e., obligations that are not grounded on our freedom) shows that freedom, by itself, is insufficient to provide moral guidance within vast domains of choice and action.

Even within the domain of freely chosen commitments and compacts, however, freedom itself fails to provide us with a compass. Knowing that a choice was free does not tell us whether it was good or morally right. One cannot choose whether something is good or right. An individual may freely join a community or withdraw from it, contribute to it or ignore it, but the features that make a community a good community and hence worth joining are not something he can freely choose. If he thinks he can decide that mutual hatred can provide a satisfactory bond between persons, he will be definitely wrong. If he admits that friendship keeps a community alive and well, he will be right. The libertarian claim that individuals should be free to form their own conception of the good doubtless is commendable, provided it is granted that some beliefs within those conceptions will be true and some false. To decide which is which, I suggest—unsurprisingly—that we need a theory of human goods such as the one offered in this book.

Conscience

I have presented brief critical sketches of utilitarianism and moral libertarianism. I have suggested that these patterns of thought, which some philosophers seek to combine, tend to pull one's judgment in opposite directions: If you emphasize utility you will find reason to restrict the freedom of some individuals, and if you press individual freedom you tend to give up general utility. I also have argued that both moral theories are inadequate because of their practical shortcomings: Both of them fail to provide satisfactory guidelines for passing moral judgment on particular actions.

Passing moral judgment on our own (future or past) actions is a function of one's conscience. The moral conscience is not a special and separate human capacity. It is an operation of practical reason (i.e., our standard capacity to think about what is good or bad). What is specific about it is the move from the universal to the particular. Instead of considering, in general, whether friendship is a basic good, conscience considers whether not showing up at a sick friend's home tonight would be, in this case, a failure in friendship and hence morally wrong.

A judgment of conscience, then, has two major components: a principle, guideline, norm, or rule that is used as a measuring rod and a description of a possible action to be measured. Both of these components can be formulated as propositions that a person believes to be true, yet both can be false. Indeed, conscience is not infallible. It can go wrong; paradoxically enough, however, we ought to do what our conscience tells us to do.

Conscience should always be followed simply because it provides the ultimate judgment one has on one's actions. If I sincerely judge that doing X would harm someone, then for me to perform that action would be consciously to violate the guideline of respect. Even if my judgment that doing X would harm someone is mistaken, I would be intentionally pursuing something that appears to me to be bad. Thus, I would violate the formal principle of practical rationality, and a feeling of guilt probably would ensue.

Feelings such as guilt are important ingredients of one's life because they often make us aware of moral failure or success. Yet feelings by themselves do not provide reliable reasons for action. It would be a mistake to let oneself be guided, say, by deeply felt bigotry or by intense hatred for someone. Feelings, like everything else, should be judged in light of the good, as perceived by one's conscience.

Not following one's conscience is the root of all hypocrisy. It amounts to thinking one thing and doing the opposite, which leads to the loss of a crucial human good: the good of integrity.

Failing in care and respect by not pursuing what one regards as good and not avoiding what one regards as bad, therefore, has a detrimental effect on one's own flourishing as a human being. Hence, it is not only morally but also prudentially mandatory to follow the dictates of one's conscience. It is both wrong and foolish not to do so.

Isn't there also folly in acting in accordance with one's conscience, if it is mistaken? There is room, indeed, for inflicting serious harm on oneself and others under an erroneous judgment of conscience, but because we have no other form of evaluating our actions, the responsible thing to do is to invest as much time and energy as one reasonably can in making sure one's conscience is not mistaken. This is easier said than done. How does one go about it? Given the ingredients of the judgment of conscience, there will be two sets of beliefs to examine.

One should subject to critical scrutiny one's general beliefs about practical rationality, basic human goods, guidelines for choice and action, and moral norms. Each plays an important role in the education of one's conscience because these are the normative principles that are brought to bear on our particular choices. One also should be aware of the corruption of conscience that can be generated, for example, by act utilitarian views that entail that sometimes we ought to do unjust deeds; one also should not lose sight of the lack of guidance for conscience that follows from a purely libertarian position.

Much of this can be done with the aid of this book. My intention in writing it was precisely to help readers form their conscience by inviting them to engage in an examination of the most general principles of practical rationality. However, reflection of a less general character also is important. Married persons would be well-advised to reaffirm their beliefs about commitment and fidelity (and their importance for the goods at stake), and health care professionals should reexamine in their own minds the principles that ought to govern their interaction with their patients (and how those principles are grounded on basic goods). For many roles and stations in life, it is possible to formulate specific rules (which can take the form of a code of professional ethics) that can help guide the individual conscience.

Conscience also can err because of a mistaken grasp of the particulars of a given case. To avoid having an erroneous conscience, then, one also should critically examine the decisive factors in trying to decide whether to do or not do something. As I argue in chapter 5, one should ask: In this case, who would be doing what and why?

The question of agency (who?) seems superfluous at first sight, but it is not. You may recall the example about Jill killing one hostage or Jack killing the rest. For the judgment of conscience, it is crucial to be clear about one's choosing to do something as opposed to someone else's doing or threatening to do something. By its very nature, conscience passes judgment on one's own actions, not on someone else's. It would not make sense for Jack to tell Jill: "My conscience tells me that it would be permissible for you to kill one hostage." Jill—and only Jill—should decide that, in accordance with the dictates of her conscience.

Second, to have a true judgment of conscience it also is necessary to frame an accurate account of the action one is about to perform (what?). To describe an act of killing one hostage as an act of saving the rest will hardly be conducive to a correct judgment of conscience because the second description can be applied to many alternative actions, some of which may violate a moral norm. If I conclude from the second description that it would be permissible for me to execute the hostage, I will have been misled into making a false judgment of conscience.

With regard to this factor, a sensible person should reflect over and over again about the main goal she would be directly intending in her choice—the one that provides a specification of the act. Is my aim to take and keep money that doesn't belong to me? Am I therefore stealing? It is easy to engage in self-deception by giving oneself muddled and evasive replies. For most people, cheating on their tax return probably takes this form.

Finally, one should critically examine one's ultimate intentions (why?) to make sure one is aiming at something good. Unintended consequences, as we have said, also should be taken into consideration, insofar as this is feasible. If one expects them to be really bad and not sufficiently compensated by the good to be achieved, one's conscience may lead one to realize that it would be immoral to proceed with the action.

Once all of this is done to the best of one's capacity—and although there is no absolute guarantee that all of one's moral beliefs will then be true—one should follow one's conscience with confidence. We will have done our best. We cannot hope for greater certainty in moral matters.

Because of the insurmountable fallibility of human conscience, one should restrict one's moral judgment of others to their overt actions, especially if the guideline of care requires intervention on one's part. One should refrain from passing a condemnatory judgment on other people as human agents. For all we know, in performing an action that is objectively wrong a person may be under the guidance of a deluded and mistaken conscience. She may sincerely believe that she is doing the right thing and thus not be morally blameworthy.

Finally, the world being as it is, one should realize that following one's conscience often requires courage. Standing up for what one believes to be the right thing or refusing to do what one honestly considers to be wrong may entail paying a high price, as Socrates did when he was executed after refusing to escape—that is, to perform an action that, as he argued, would have been unjust and unfair to his political community. Courage also is required to admit one's fault when, unlike Socrates, one fails to live up to the standards of morality.

Notes

1. Smart and Williams (1988), 71.
2. Griffin (1988), 67.
3. Pettit (1993), xv–xvi.
4. Finnis (1980), 155.
5. Grisez and Boyle (1979), 39–44.

APPENDIX:

Explanations and Sources

Natural Law

The first point demanding explanation is why a book that professes to provide an introduction to natural law ethics does not contain appeals to nature as a whole or, more specifically, to human nature to justify its normative claims, as the standard picture of the doctrine seems to demand.[1] The traditional expression "natural law" in the subtitle is meant first and foremost to draw a contrast with the notion of "civic law"[2] or, more broadly, "human law."[3]

In antiquity, a city-state (in Greek *polis*, in Latin *civitas*) enacted laws as it deemed necessary for its own welfare. Its laws were *civic*— that is, peculiar to a given city and enforceable within its walls. They lacked force elsewhere.

Different states, in the past and in the present, pass different laws, but all of those laws originate in exactly the same way: They are human-made or "posited" by humans and thus jointly constitute what is called human or positive law.

It is matter of human law that cars should be driven on the right or the left side of the road, and not all countries have chosen the same solution for the coordination and safety of traffic. The choice a country makes is an agreement (convention, contract) made by its legislators.[4] Which agreement they reach is a matter of indifference, as long as it manages to avoid accidents and preserve lives.

That life is a basic good, by contrast, is not the result of a convention, nor is it true only in some countries. Hence, that human life should be preserved and, furthermore, that it is wrong to murder people is not a conventional norm that binds solely within the frontiers of some states and not others. It is a requirement of practical reason, something in which all mankind shares. Thus, it is "natural" and not merely "civic"—in the same way that "fire burns both here and in Persia," as Aristotle remarked.[5] Murder is wrong for the same reasons everywhere, and civic law ought to reflect that.

To claim, then, that there is a normative domain governed by "natural law" is to claim that there is a common moral order that is not subject to particular human agreements or conventions. It is not posited or decided by mankind. It has to be discovered.

This does not imply any confusion between the normative notion of natural law and the laws of nature explored by the natural sciences. The latter express the regularities that are pervasive in the world and are purely descriptive. No prescriptive conclusions for human action can be drawn from, say, the laws of physics or chemistry or from the behavior of animals.

Exploration into natural law (though not under this name, at first) was initiated by Socrates and other Greek thinkers who attempted to identify the human goods—the set of goods that provide the foundation for the objective moral order.[6] Among those thinkers, only the Stoics defended strong connections between nature and the human good,[7] though the exact import of their conception is a matter of scholarly debate.[8] Although Stoic elements do play a significant role in later natural law thinking, it is fair to say that Aristotle is the philosopher who provides the basic framework for the classical version of the doctrine, the one put forward by St. Thomas Aquinas. As I have argued elsewhere, however, it is a mistake to think that Aristotle makes an inference from human nature to the human good or happiness, the cornerstone of his moral philosophy. A detailed analysis of the key argument in the *Nicomachean Ethics* shows that that is not the case.[9]

The first reason, then, to reject the view that any credible version of natural law ethics is committed to drawing normative inferences from human nature or from nature as a whole is that "natural" within the label points primarily to the view that certain norms are common to mankind, and that they are not crafted by man. There is a second reason for thinking that such inferences are neither necessary nor possible. This reason is grounded on the very principles of practical reason.

According to Aquinas, the principles of practical reason are *per se nota omnibus*, "known through themselves to all."[10] They are not *per aliud nota:* They do not need something else, a middle term, to be shown to be true. They need not, and cannot, be proved. They are self-evident in this sense (not in the sense of being instantly obvious).

The self-evidence of the first principle of practical reason ("what is good ought to be pursued, what is bad avoided") can be explained as the self-evidence of an analytic *a priori* proposition in the modern sense.[11] It is by virtue of understanding what the words "good" and "bad" mean in ordinary language that anyone can know it to be true. This is the view taken in chapter 2, but it does not rule out an Aristotelian interpretation according to which "good" stands for an intelligible content (a *noetón*) that is directly grasped by the mind.

The self-evidence of the supplementary principles is different. Experience such as that provided by everyday life (with a modicum of reflection on the corresponding concept) is required to realize, for example, that friendship is good, but no third concept is needed to establish a link between friendship and its goodness. There is no room for it. Thus, the proposition may be said to be analytic, but it is known *a posteriori*. That water has one atom of oxygen in its molecule also is analytic; it also is known *a posteriori* because observation and experiment were required to establish that water is H_2O.

A grasp of human nature that demands sophisticated intellectual training to be understood would not provide proof that friendship is a basic good; it would assume it. That man is endowed with a natural capacity for friendship (or has a natural inclination to sociability) would have to be derived from our realization that it is good to have friends, not the other way around. Indeed, it is not because we have an inclination to X that we may infer that X is good for us. It is our prior grasp of X as good that justifies the claim that our inclination to X is a *natural* inclination. The appeal to natural inclinations is part of the theoretical enterprise to understand our nature, but it does not have a foundational role in the practical enterprise.[12]

A related point is implied in Aquinas' clarification that the practical principles are accessible to all (*omnibus*), not only to the wise (*solis sapientibus*). The wise are metaphysicians and theologians who do have an adequate grasp of human nature. If practical principles were known to be true by virtue of an inference from human nature, knowledge of natural law would be severely restricted to a small segment of society. Most people could then excuse themselves from the claims of morality because its starting points would lie beyond their lights.

What I have tried to do is to develop a system of pure practical reason starting from self-evident, practical principles that anyone can understand and accept. By calling it "a system of *pure practical reason*," I seek to emphasize that this book contains no foundational claims that are based on faith or, alternatively, on theoretical reason. No appeals are made to theological or metaphysical truths about God, nature, or the essence of human beings to ground normative principles, guidelines, or norms.

Perhaps my treatment of the good of knowledge can readily illustrate the resolve to remain strictly within the domain of practical reason alone. In asking the reader to accept that knowledge is a basic human good, I do not seek prior assent to the claim that human beings have by nature an inclination to know or that God created us to know Him through His creatures. I simply invite the reader to realize that any effort to deny that knowledge is good presupposes the realization that it would be good to know and that one is better off knowing than remaining in ignorance or error. I took it that any reasonable person would grant this, as well as the fundamental importance of knowledge for a truly flourishing life.

At one point, however, a brief theoretical treatment of key ingredients of human action (chapter 5) turns out to be unavoidable, not because its results would justify certain actions but only because awareness of those ingredients (Who? What? Why?) allows us better to understand how moral judgments should be framed. The main reason to refrain from appealing to purely theoretical premises is the well-known (and logically well-grounded) doctrine that no practical (i.e., evaluative) conclusion can follow validly from premises that do not contain evaluations.[13]

Theological truths are excluded for a different reason. Practical conclusions can be drawn validly from suitable theological premises, but the faith required to give assent to those premises is a gift, and one cannot expect everyone to have it. Exclusion of theological claims, however, does not generate inconsistencies between the doctrines they would justify and the views defended here. In fact, everything held in this book is consistent, to the best of my knowledge, with mainstream

Judeo-Christian ethics and, in particular, with Roman Catholic teaching. My overall aim, then, is to present a version of common, natural law morality that, insofar as it is based exclusively on reason, is accessible to anyone and therefore is binding on everyone without distinction.

Sources

A project of this nature relies unavoidably on many and varied sources. Among the remote ones, the most important are the writings of Plato and Aristotle and the fragments of the Stoics. Although Aquinas plays a decisive role within the natural law tradition, there is surprisingly little on it in his voluminous works. The key passage is *Summa Theologiae* I–II, q. 94, a. 2, which should be read together with the ground-breaking commentary by Germain Grisez.[14]

The immediate impulse to write this book came from years of use of Alan Donagan's *The Theory of Morality*[15] in the teaching of ethics. Donagan provides a valuable exposition of traditional morality that makes excellent use of historical sources and contemporary material, although his final choice of a Kantian fundamental principle proves to be disappointing. Respect for persons is of paramount importance in the conduct of one's life, but it sometimes fails to provide firm guidelines for deciding particular issues. Is physician-assisted suicide an instance of respect or disrespect for persons? After some time, I became convinced that respect for persons should be understood as respect for the goods of persons and that therefore a system of human goods is preferable in the task of accounting for morality.

Although this book tries to emulate Donagan's, in content it is much closer to *Natural Law and Natural Rights* by John Finnis.[16] My debt to Finnis should be obvious on every page of this book. To him I owe much of the overall structure and the insistence on starting exclusively from self-evident practical principles, thereby blocking the oft-repeated objection that natural law ethics is based on a fallacious inference from fact to value. My list of goods and guidelines departs somewhat from Finnis', and he addresses some topics (such as jurisprudence) that I do not discuss.

I also have learned quite a bit from many books and articles by philosophers with whose views I disagree. The list would be long and its presence here otiose because most of their works appear in the bibliography.

Notes

1. Wollheim (1967).
2. This basic understanding of the terminology owes much to the Roman jurists whose views are summarized in the opening sections of Emperor Justinian's *Digest* (sixth century A.D.). See also Aristotle *Rhetoric* 1.13.1373b4–6. On the ancient and medieval sources, see Ricken (1994).
3. Aquinas *Summa Theologiae* I–II, q. 90, a. 3.
4. Aristotle *Rhetoric* 1.15.1376b9–10.
5. Aristotle *Nicomachean Ethics* 5.7.1134b26.
6. Gómez-Lobo (1994), 95–96.
7. Diogenes Laertius 7.87–89. See Long and Sedley (1987), I. 395 and 400; Donagan (1977), 1–4.
8. See Schofield and Striker (1986) and Annas (1993), 159–87.
9. Gómez-Lobo (1989).
10. Aquinas *Summa Theologiae* I–II, q. 94, a. 2. The doctrine itself is Aristotelian, and its formulation assumes that syllogistic inference requires a middle term to justify attributing the predicate to the subject. That Socrates is mortal is proved to be true because there is a middle term, being human, that is true of Socrates and of which it is true that all members of its class are bound to die.
11. I have borrowed the terms "analytic *a priori*" and "analytic *a posteriori*" from Kripke (1977) as useful labels for the present purposes. They require independent justification, of course.
12. There are distinguished representatives of the natural law tradition who would dispute this and argue that human nature or nature in general does play a grounding role in the practical domain. See Veatch (1971), McInerny (1982), and Hittinger (1987).
13. Hare (1975), 27–31.
14. Grisez (1965).
15. Donagan (1977).
16. Finnis (1980).

SELECTED BIBLIOGRAPHY

Annas, J. 1993. *The Morality of Happiness.* New York: Oxford University Press.

Aristotle 1984. *The Complete Works of Aristotle*, 2 vol., edited by J. Barnes. Princeton, N.J.: Princeton University Press.

Augustine. 1993. *On Free Choice of the Will.* Indianapolis: Hackett.

Beauchamp, T. L., and J. F. Childress. 1989. *Principles of Biomedical Ethics.* 3d ed. New York: Oxford University Press.

———. 1994. *Principles of Biomedical Ethics.* 4th ed. New York: Oxford University Press.

Brandt, R. B. 1967. "Hedonism." In *The Encyclopedia of Philosophy,* Vol. 3, edited by P. Edwards. New York: Macmillan.

Chappell, T. D. J. 1998. *Understanding Human Goods.* Edinburgh: Edinburgh University Press.

Donagan, A. 1977. *The Theory of Morality.* Chicago: University of Chicago Press.

———. 1987. *Choice. The Essential Element in Human Action.* London: Routledge and Kegan Paul.

Emanuel, L. L., ed. 1998. *Regulating How We Die. The Ethical, Medical, and Legal Issues Surrounding Physician-Assisted Suicide.* Cambridge, Mass.: Harvard University Press.

English, J. 1997. "Abortion and the Concept of a Person." In *Contemporary Moral Problems,* 5th ed., edited by J. E. White (Minneapolis, Minn.: West, 1997), 151–58. First published in *Canadian Journal of Philosophy* 5 (1975): 233–43.

Fagothey, A., S.J. 1976. *Right and Reason: Ethics in Theory and Practice.* 6th ed. St. Louis: Mosby.

Feinberg, J. 1986. "Abortion." In *Matters of Life and Death: New Introductory Essays in Moral Philosophy,* 2d ed., edited by T. Regan (New York: Random House, 1986), 256–93.

Feinberg, J., and Levenbook, B. B. 1993. "Abortion." In *Matters of Life and Death: New Introductory Essays in Moral Philosophy,* 3d ed., edited by T. Regan (New York: Random House, 1993), 195–234.

Finnis, J. 1980. *Natural Law and Natural Rights.* New York: Oxford University Press.

Gert, B. 1988. *Morality: A New Justification of the Moral Norms.* New York: Oxford University Press.

Gomez, C. F. 1991. *Regulating Death: Euthanasia and the Case of the Netherlands.* New York: Free Press.

Gómez-Lobo, A. 1985. "Natural Law and Naturalism." *Proceedings of the American Catholic Philosophical Association,* 59:232–49.

———. 1989. "The Ergon Inference." *Phronesis* 34:170–84.

———. 1994. *The Foundations of Socratic Ethics.* Indianapolis, Ind.: Hackett.

Griffin, J. 1988. *Well-Being: Its Meaning, Measurement and Moral Importance.* Oxford: Oxford University Press.

Grisez, G. 1965. "The First Principle of Practical Reason. A Commentary on *Summa Theologiae* 1–2, Question 94, Article 2." *Natural Law Forum* 10:168–201.

Grisez, G., and J. M. Boyle. 1979. *Life and Death with Liberty and Justice: A Contribution to the Euthanasia Debate.* Notre Dame, Ind.: University of Notre Dame Press.

Hare, R. M. 1975. *The Language of Morals.* Oxford: Oxford University Press.

Hittinger, R 1987. *A Critique of the New Natural Law Theory.* Notre Dame, Ind.: University of Notre Dame Press.

Kenny, A., ed. 1969. *Aquinas: A Collection of Critical Essays.* Garden City, N.Y.: Anchor Books.

Kripke, S. 1977. "Identity and Necessity." In *Naming, Necessity, and Natural Kinds,* edited by S. P. Schwartz (Ithaca, N.Y.: Cornell University Press, 1977), 66–101.

Long, A. A., and D. N. Sedley. 1987. *The Hellenistic Philosophers.* 2 vol. Cambridge: Cambridge University Press.

Mackie, J. L. 1986. *Ethics: Inventing Right and Wrong.* Harmondsworth, U.K.: Penguin Books.

McInerny, R. 1982. *Ethica Thomistica: The Moral Philosophy of Thomas Aquinas.* Washington, D.C.: Catholic University of America Press.

Mill, J. S. 1978. *On Liberty.* Indianapolis, Ind.: Hackett.

———. 1979. *Utilitarianism.* Indianapolis, Ind.: Hackett.

Murphy, M. 1997. "The Conscience Principle." *Journal of Philosophical Research* 22:387–407.

Noonan, J. T., ed. 1977. *The Morality of Abortion: Legal and Historical Perspectives.* Cambridge, Mass.: Harvard University Press.

Oderberg, D. S. 2000a. *Moral Theory: A Non-Consequentialist Approach.* Oxford: Blackwell.

————. 2000b. *Applied Ethics: A Non-Consequentialist Approach.* Oxford: Blackwell.

Pellegrino, E. 1998. "The False Promise of Beneficent Killing." In *Regulating How We Die: The Ethical, Moral, and Legal Issues Surrounding Physician-Assisted Suicide,* edited by L. Emanuel (Cambridge, Mass.: Harvard University Press, 1998), 71–91.

Pettit, P., ed. 1993. *Consequentialism.* Aldershot, Vt.: Dartmouth Publishing Co.

Plato. 1997. *Complete Works,* edited by J. M. Cooper and D. S. Hutchinson. Indianapolis, Ind.: Hackett.

Powers, M. 1995. "Contemporary Defenses of the Doctrine of Double Effect." *Revue Internationale de Philosophie* 193:341–56.

Rachels, J. 1986. *The End of Life: Euthanasia and Morality.* Oxford: Oxford University Press.

————. 1993. "Euthanasia." In *Matters of Life and Death: New Introductory Essays in Moral Philosophy,* edited by T. Regan (New York: Random House, 1993), 30–68.

————. 1999a. *The Right Thing to Do: Basic Readings in Moral Philosophy.* 2d ed. Boston: McGraw-Hill.

————. 1999b. "The Morality of Euthanasia." In *The Right Thing to Do,* 190–94; selected from *Matters of Life and Death: New Introductory Essays in Moral Philosophy,* 2d ed., edited by T. Regan (New York: Random House, 1986).

Rawls, J. 1971. *A Theory of Justice.* Cambridge, Mass.: Harvard University Press.

Regan, T. 1983. *The Case for Animal Rights.* Berkeley: University of California Press.

————, ed. 1986. *Matters of Life and Death: New Introductory Essays in Moral Philosophy.* 2d ed. New York: Random House.

————, ed. 1993. *Matters of Life and Death: New Introductory Essays in Moral Philosophy.* 3d ed. New York: Random House.

Ricken, F. 1994. "Naturrecht I." *Theologische Realenzyklopädie,* 24, no. 1/2:132–53.

Sandbach, F. H. 1989. *The Stoics.* 2d ed. Indianapolis, Ind.: Hackett.

Schofield, M., and G. Striker, eds. 1986. *The Norms of Nature.* New York: Cambridge Univesity Press.

Schwartz, S. P., ed. 1977. *Naming, Necessity, and Natural Kinds.* Ithaca, N.Y.: Cornell University Press.

Sen, A., and B. Williams, eds. 1988. *Utilitarianism and Beyond.* Cambridge: Cambridge University Press.

Singer, P. 1975. *Animal Liberation. A New Ethics for Our Treatment of Animals.* New York: New York Review.

———. 1993. "Animals and the Value of Life." In *Matters of Life and Death: New Introductory Essays in Moral Philosophy,* edited by T. Regan (New York: Random House, 1993), 280–321.

Smart, J. J. C., and B. Williams. 1988. *Utilitarianism: For and Against.* Cambridge: Cambridge University Press.

Sulmasy, D. P. 1998. "Killing and Allowing to Die: Another Look." *Journal of Law, Medicine and Ethics* 26:55–64.

Thomas Aquinas. 1988a. Sancti Thomae de Aquino. *Summa Theologiae.* Mediolani, Italy: Editiones Paulinae.

———. 1988b. *On Politics and Ethics. A New Translation, Backgrounds, Interpretations,* edited by P. E. Sigmund. New York: Norton.

Thomson, J. J. 1997. "A Defense of Abortion." In *Contemporary Moral Problems,* 5th ed., edited by J. E. White (Minneapolis, Minn.: West, 1997), 122–31. First published in *Philosophy and Public Affairs* 1 (1971):47–66.

Tooley, M. 1972. "Abortion and Infanticide." *Philosophy and Public Affairs* 2:37–65.

Veatch, H. 1971. *For an Ontology of Morals: A Critique of Contemporary Ethical Theory.* Evanston, Ill.: Northwestern University Press.

Warren, M . A. 1997. "On the Moral and Legal Status of Abortion." In *Contemporary Moral Problems,* 5th ed., edited by J. E. White (Minneapolis, Minn.: West, 1997), 131–43. First published in *The Monist* 57 (1973):43–61.

White, J. E. 1997. *Contemporary Moral Problems.* 5th ed. Minneapolis: West.

Wollheim, R. 1967. "Natural Law." In *The Encyclopedia of Philosophy,* Vol. 5, edited by P. Edwards. New York: Macmillan.

INDEX